MACRAMÉ FOR

JEWELRY

Easy to Follow Step-by-Step Guide to Create Original
and Unique Bracelets, Earrings, and Accessories

30+ Illustrated Handmade Projects

Natalie Holder

Table of Contents

Introduction

Macramé is a practice that has lasted for thousands of years. The textile industry has held on to this form of art for a pretty long time. As the world evolved, there also arose a need to scale the degree of macramé to a large extent so that it can still find application in today's world and remain relevant. Many innovations have started taking the idea of macramé beyond just plant and wall hangers. Macramé can likewise be used to produce, among many other things, like key chains and table runners.

Materials commonly used for macramé are cotton yarn, hemp, leather, or yarn. While there are variations, the main knots are the square knot, the full suspension, and the double half. Jewelry is often made by combining buttons with pearls, shells, rings, or gems. If you look at most of the friend bracelets worn by school children, you will see that they are made of macramé.

Jewelry Projects

Serenity Bracelet

(**Note:** if you are familiar with the flat knot, you can move right along into the next pattern) This novice bracelet offers plenty of practice using one of the micro macramé's most used knots. You will also gain experience in beading and equalizing tension. This bracelet features a button closure, and the finished length is 7 inches.

Knot Used:

- Flat Knot (aka square knot)

- Overhand knot

Materials:

- White C-Lon cord, 6 ½ ft., x 3

- 18 - Frosted Purple size 6 beads

- 36 - Purple seed beads, size 11

- 1 - 1 cm Purple and white focal bead

- 26 - Dark Purple size 6 beads

- 1 - 5 mm Purple button closure bead

(*Note:* the button bead needs to be able to fit into all 6 cords)

Take all 3 cords and fold them in half. Find the center and place on your

work surface as shown:

Now hold the cords and tie an overhand knot, loosely, at the center

point. It should look like this:

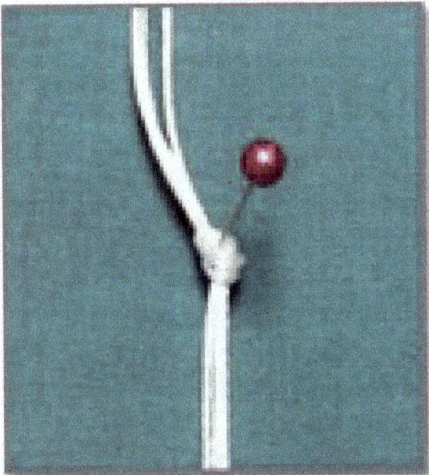

1. We will now make a buttonhole closure. Just below the knot, take each outer cord and tie a flat knot (aka square knot). Continue tying flat knots until you have about 2 ½ cm.

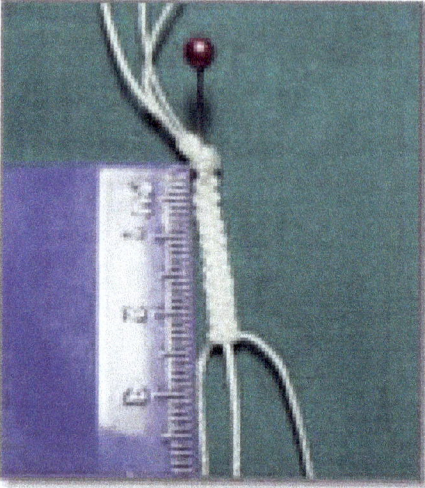

2. Undo your overhand knot and place the ends together in a horseshoe shape.

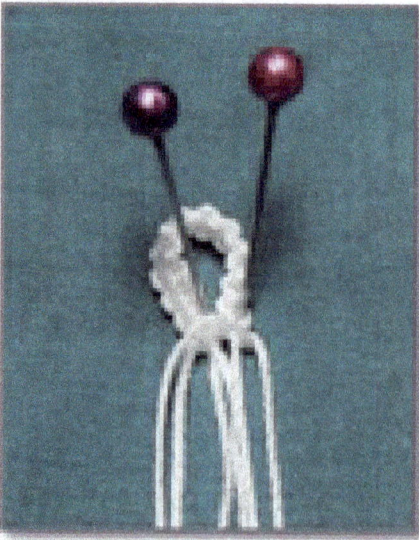

3. We now have all 6 cords together. Think of the cords as numbered 1 through 6 from left to right. Cords 2-5 will stay in the middle as filler cords. Find cord 1 and 6 and use these to tie flat knots around the filler cords. (Note: now you can pass your button bead through the opening to ensure a good fit. Add or subtract flat knots as needed to create a snug fit. This size should be fine for a 5mm bead). Continue to tie flat knots until you have 4 cm worth. (To increase bracelet length, add more flat knots here and the equal amount in step 10).

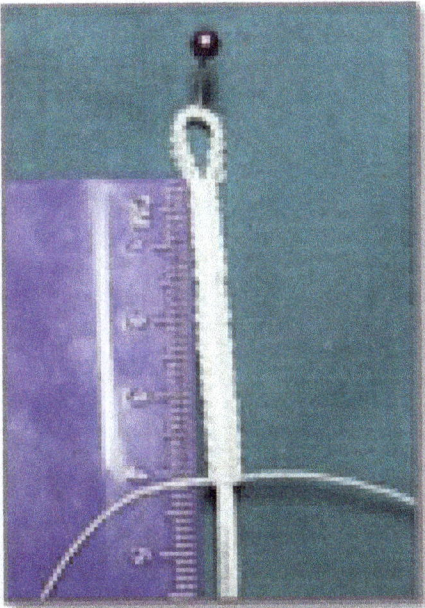

4. Separate cords 1-4-1. Find the center 2 cords. Thread a size 6 frosted purple bead onto them, then tie a flat knot with cords 2 and 5.

5. We will now work with cords 1 and 6. With cord 1, thread on a seed bead, a dark purple size 6 beads, and another seed bead. Repeat with cord 6, and then separate the cords into 3-3. Tie a flat knot with the left 3 cords. Tie a flat knot with the right 3 cords.

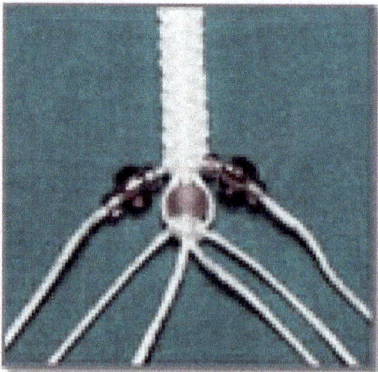
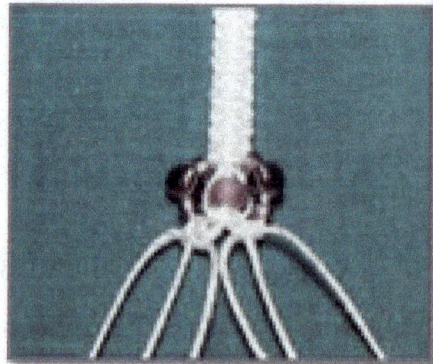

6. Repeat step 4 and 5 three times.

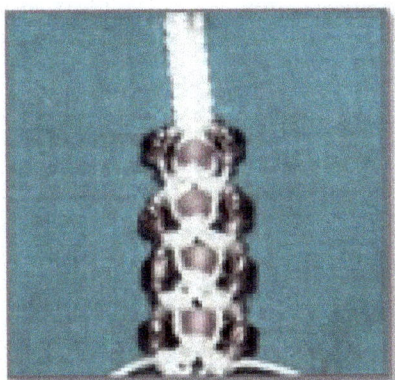

7. Find the center 2 cords, hold together, and thread on the 1cm focal bead. Take the next cords out (2 and 5) and bead as follows: 2 size 6 dark purple beads, a frosted purple bead, and 2 dark purple beads. Find cords 1 and 6 and bead as follows: 2 frosted purple beads, a seed bead, a dark

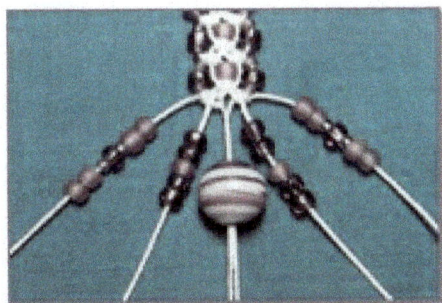

purple bead, a seed bead, 2 frosted purple beads.

8. With cords 2 and 5, tie a flat knot around the center 2 cords. Place the center 4 cords together and tie a flat knot around them with outer cords 1 and 6.

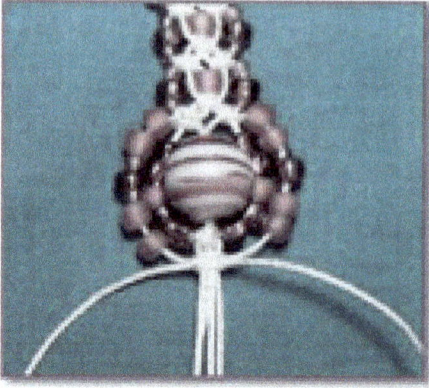

9. Repeat steps 4 and 5 four times.

10. Repeat step 3.

11. Place your button bead on all 6 cords and tie an overhand knot tight against the bead. Glue well and trim the cords.

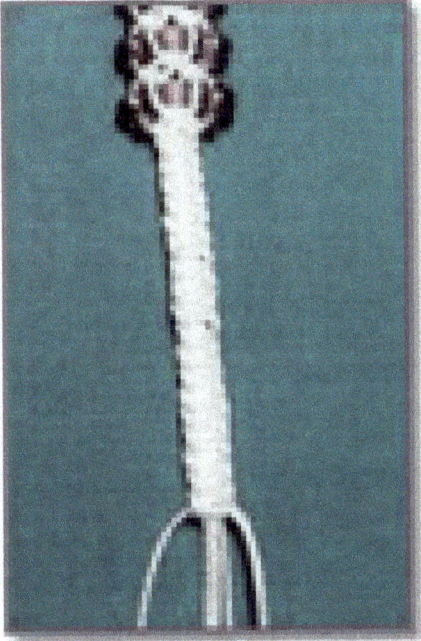

Lantern Bracelet

This pattern may look simple, but please don't try it if you are in a hurry. This one takes patience. Don't worry about getting your picot knots all the exact same shape. Have fun with it! The finished bracelet is 7 ¼ inches in length. If desired, add a picot knot and a spiral knot on each side of the centerpiece to lengthen it. This pattern has a jump ring closure.

Knots Used:

- Spiral Knot

- Picot Knot

- Overhand Knot

Materials:

- 3 strands of C-Lon cord (2 light brown and 1 medium brown) 63-inch lengths

- Fasteners (1 jump ring, 1 spring ring or lobster clasp)

- 8 small beads (about 4mm) amber to gold colors

- 30 gold seed beads

- 3 beads (about 6 mm) amber color (mine are rectangular, but round or oval will work wonderfully also)

Note: Bead size can vary slightly. Just be sure all beads you choose will slide onto 2 cords (except seed beads).

1. Find the center of your cord and attach it to the jump ring with a knot. Repeat with the 2 remaining strands. If you want the 2-tone effect, be sure your second color is NOT placed in the center, or it will only be a filler cord, and you will end up with a 1 tone bracelet.

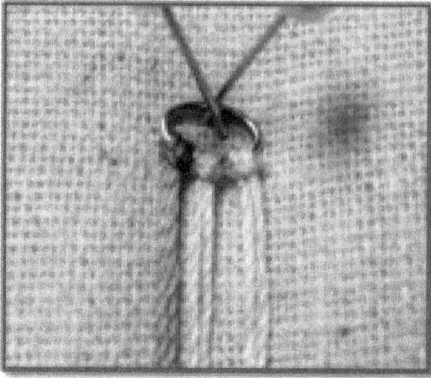

2. You now have 6 cords to work with. Think of them as numbers 1 to 6, from left to right. Move cords 1 and 6 apart from the rest. You will use these to work the spiral knot. All others are filler cords. Take cord number 1 and tie a spiral knot. Always begin with the left cord. Tie 7 more spirals.

3. Place a 4mm bead on the center 2 cords. Leave cords 1 and 6 alone for now and work 1 flat knot using cords 2 and 5.

4. Now put cords 2 and 5 together with the center strands. Use 1 and 6 to tie a picot flat knot. If you don't like the look of your picot knot, loosen it up and try again. Gently tug the cords into place, then lock in tightly with the next spiral knot.

Notice here how I am holding the picot knot with my thumbs while pulling the cords tight with my fingers. If you look closely, you may be able to see that I have a cord in each hand.

5. Tie 8 spiral knots (using left cord throughout pattern).

6. Place a 4mm bead on the center 2 cords. Leave cords 1 and 6 alone for now and work 1 flat knot using cords 2 and 5. Now put cords 2 and 5 together with the center strands. Use strands 1 and 6 to tie a picot flat knot.

7. Repeat steps 5 and 6 until you have 5 sets of spirals.

8. Then place 5 seed beads on cords 1 and 6. Put cords 3 and 4 together and string on a 6 mm bead. Tie one flat knot with the outermost cords.

Repeat this step two more times.

Now repeat steps 5 and 6 until you have 5 sets of spirals from the center point. Thread on your clasp. Tie an overhand knot with each cord and glue well. Let dry completely. As this is the weakest point in the design, I advise to trim the excess cords and gluing again. Let dry.

Zig Zag Bracelet

Materials:

• 60cm length of 2mm black waxed cotton cord

• 150cm length of 2mm black waxed cotton cord

• 16 8mm oval beads (must have a 2mm hole minimum)

• 1 15mm disk bead or button with central hole (minimum hole diameter of 4mm) Tools List

• Macramé board and Pins (optional)

• Scissors

• Clear nail varnish (optional)

• PVA glue

Steps:

Step 1 - Fold the shorter length of cord in half and place it round a pin on your macramé board, if using. If not just lay the cord on a flat surface.

Step 2 - Fold the longer length of cord in half and tie one square knot around the shorter cords.

This knot needs to be placed so that the loop created in the end of the shorter cords is a tight fit for the disk bead to fit through.

Step 3 - Tie a further four square knots.

Step 4 - Thread eight beads on to each of the central cords.

Step 5 - Pick up the longer cord on the right and take it across the central cord, under the first bead and then under the central cords so it come out back on the right side under the first bead on the right side

central cord.

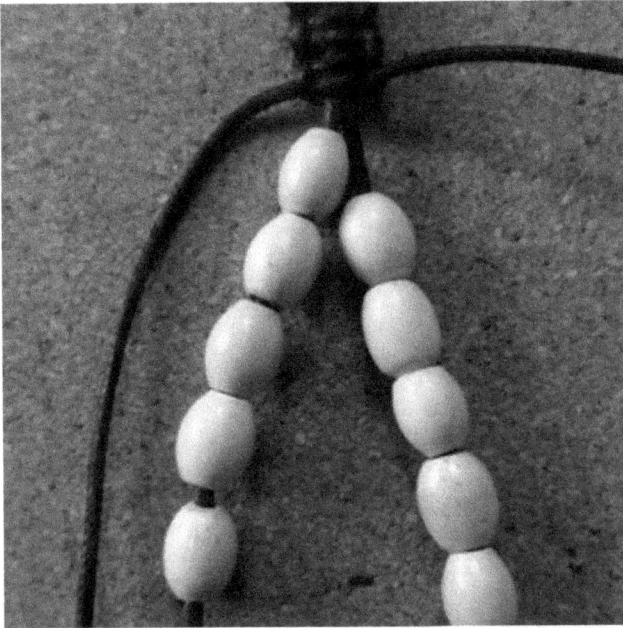

Step 6 - Repeat step 5 until you have wrapped the right cord around all the beads, moving the beads into place as you go.

Step 7 - Holding the right cord in place at the bottom of the beads, repeat steps 5 and 6 using the left side longer cord.

Step 8 - Now tie one square knot to secure the wrapped cords.

Step 9 - Tie another four square knots to match the ones at the start of the bracelet.

Step 10 - Cut off the excess long outer cord lengths and cover the ends and surrounding area with PVA glue. The glue will secure the ends and dries clear so will not show. Allow the glue to dry.

Thread the disk bead onto the two centrals cord and leaving a gap of a few millimetres, tie an overhand knot to secure. After cutting off the excess cord in step 11, the ends can be dipped into clear nail varnish if desired. Once dry this will stop the cord from fraying.

Pizzaz Anklet

Materials:

- C-Lon cord, 5 ft 6 in., Rose (x1), Mint (x1), Apricot (x1)
- 5mm button bead (x1)
- Light green size 11 seed beads (x108)
- Pink size 11 seed beads (x64)
- Light pink size 6 seed beads (x40)
- Beacon 527 glue

Steps:

Place all 3 cords together and find the center. Tie a loose overhand knot at the center point and place the cords on your project board as shown with the green on the left and the pink on the right:

Using the outer most cord on each side, tie about 10 flat knots around the inner cords. Untie the overhand knot and place the flat knots in a horseshoe shape. Pin the ends in place and check to see if your button bead will fit (snugly) through the opening. Adjust flat knots as necessary.

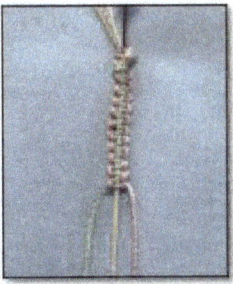

Rearrange the cords so that both green cords are on the left, the apricot cords are in the center and both pink cords are on the right. Using the outer cord on each side (green and a pink) tie a flat knot.

Separate the cords 2-2-2. Find the second cord in from each side and thread on 3 size 11 light green seed beads.

Take the left apricot cord and tie a VLH knot onto the beaded cord to the left of it. Tug gently on the apricot cord to form an arc. Now take the right apricot cord and thread it through the arc, then tie a VLH knot onto the beaded cord to the right. Tug gently on the apricot cord to form an arc.

Find the left cord (green) and attach it to the beaded green cord with a VLH knot. Tug gently to create an arc to the outside. Repeat with the right cord (pink onto pink).

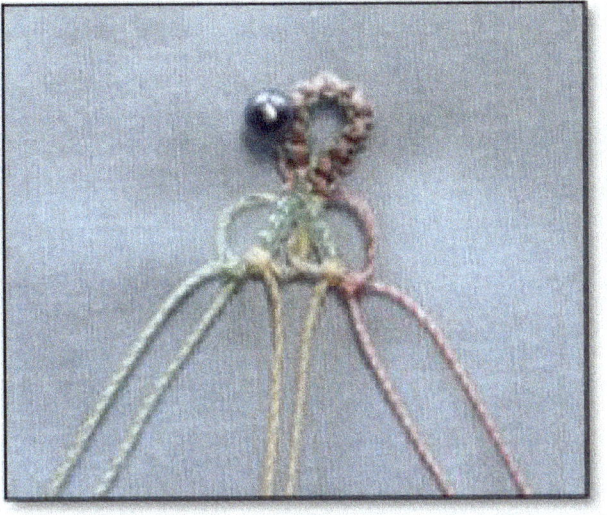

Repeat steps 4-6, then tie a flat knot with the outer cord on each side.
Note: As you go on, if the left green cord is getting too short, swap it
with the longer green cord next to it either before or after this flat knot.

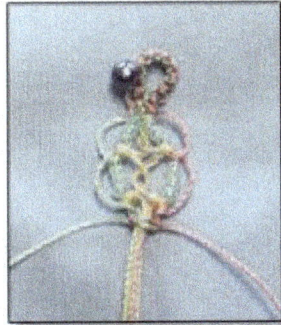

Take the left cord and thread on four size 11 pink seed beads, one size 6 pale pink seed bead and another four size 11 pink seed beads, then set it aside. Find the right cord (pink) and place it to the left, over the other 4 cords, as the holding cord (HC). Tie diagonal double half hitch (DDHH) knots onto it from right to left.

Find the right cord and thread onto it three pale pink size 6 beads. Skip the next cord in and place on the next cord a size 6 pale pink bead.

Take the HC from the left and place it to the right. Tie DDHH knots onto it from left to right. Retrieve the set aside cord and use it along with the far right cord to tie a flat knot around the other cords.Repeat steps 4 through 10 until you have reached 9 1/2 inches. With the center 2 cords, thread 2 or 4 cords through the button bead. Use the remaining cords to tie a flat knot around it. Glue the back of the flat knot and let dry. Then trim the cords and glue once more.

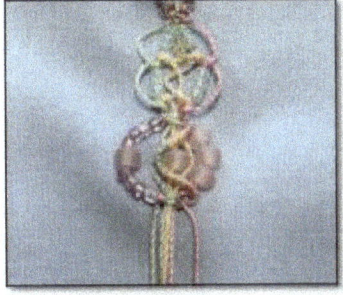

For this one you can use Teal, Blue Lagoon and Amethyst cord

Silky Purple Necklace

This silky necklace looks quite regal as it is in the color of purple. With the help of rhinestones, it becomes all the more elegant!

What you need:

- Rhinestones
- Clasp
- 2 inches of chain
- Thread and needle (in the same color scheme)
- 6 yards silk rattail cord

Instructions:

Cut string into 6 yards, and the other to be 36 inches. Make sure that you loop the last chain link.

Make use of square knots to tie the outer cord with the inner cord, and make sure to overlap on the left. Bring the string's end right under the center strings. Knot by pulling the right and left ends of the cord.

Repeat the process on the opposite side of the chain and make sure to pull tight through the loop and make use of square knots until you reach your desired length.

Double knot the cord once you read your desired length so you could lock it up. Make use of fabric glue to secure the ends of the cord together.

Attach rhinestones with glue and let dry before using.

Enjoy your new necklace!

Macramé Necklace

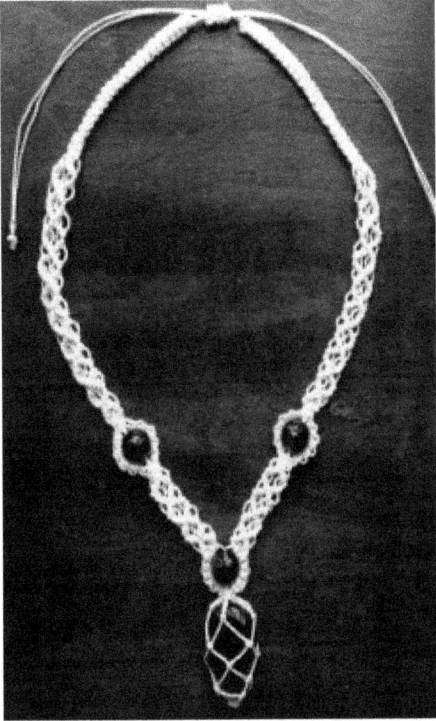

Tools and Supplies:

- Six strands each approximately 4 to 5 feet in length for a total of around ten yards 1 mm Waxed polyester cord

- One inch long tumbled amethyst stone

- Three 8mm round amethyst beads

- 2 small beads of glass

Step 1

Set aside 2 of your cords. Take the remaining four and begin by creating a macramé net/stone wrap. Create 3 flat knots (1,5 square knots) or a gourmand pattern below the wrap. Slide a bead through 2 middle cords.

Step 2

Take 3 strands from one side of your bead. Use 2 of the strands as a base, then use the 3rd to create a sennit of Lark's head knot. Ensure that your loops are outward-facing. This pattern created five larks head knot, which is adequate for looping around the bead (according to your bead size, you may require more or less). Mount 1 of the cords which you had

set aside earlier onto the threads at the base.

Step 3

Using one of the strands that you had pulled through your bead, create a double half hitch on the threads at the base.

Step 4

Rework steps three to five on the second side. Take the 6 cords to the left and use them to create a diamond pattern. This pattern formed three, five diamonds. Complete with three flat knots (1,5 SK).

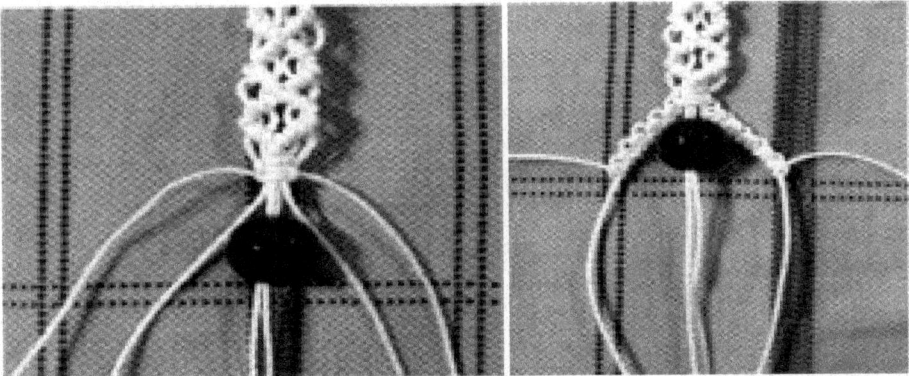

Step 5

Slide a bead through 2 center cords. Create sennits of lark's head/ frioille knots on either side of your beads.

Step 6

Create 3 more flat knots (1,5 SKs) on the underside.

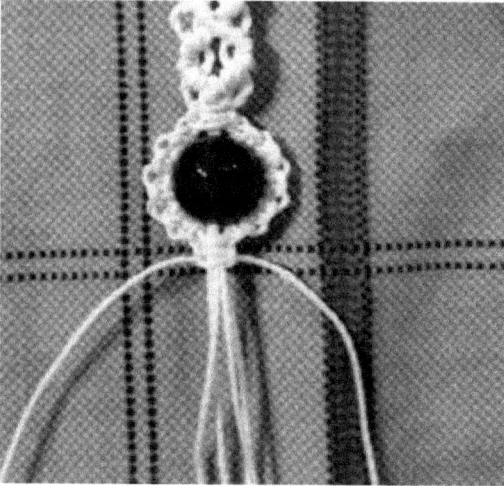

Step 7

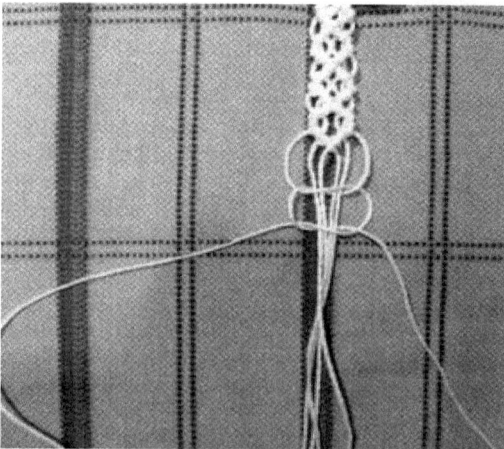

Proceed using the diamond design. This pattern created ten "diamonds" – you can create less or more according to your preferred necklace length.

Step 8

Weave a braid of square knots that is a couple of inches long; for this pattern, it was 2.5 inches.

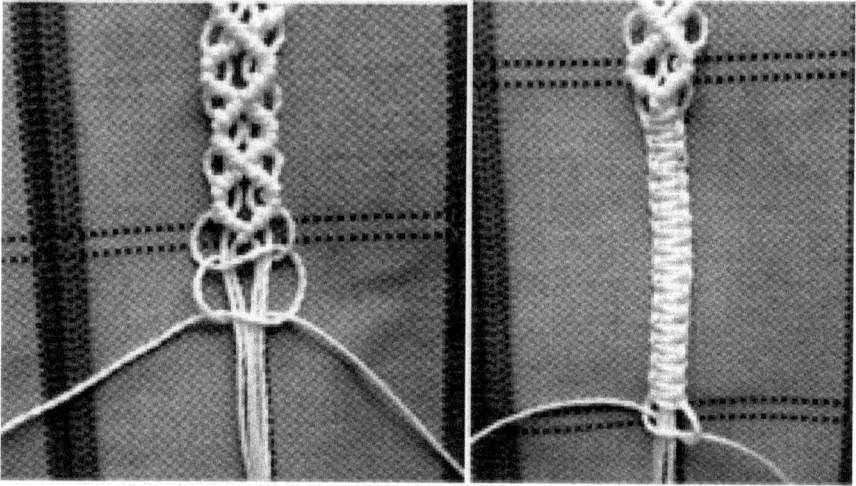

Step 9

Switch your necklace to the converse side, then use the working strands to create an overhand knot. Clip off the strands and apply a bit of glue to your knot.

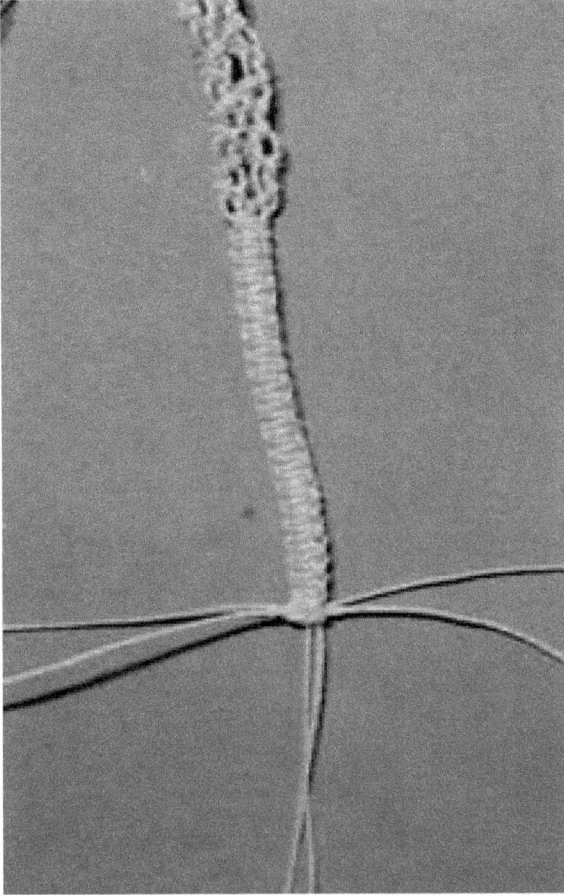

Step 10

Cut the cords at the base to your preferred length (five to six inches), then pull the small beads through the cords. At the tip of every strand, create a simple knot.

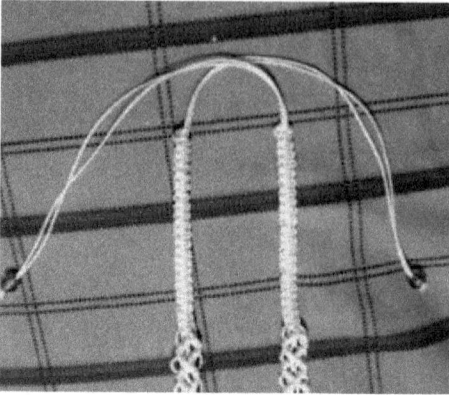

Step 11

Form a clasp closure that can be adjusted. Do this by placing a strand that is two to three inches in length below the strands at the base and then tie five to six SKs.

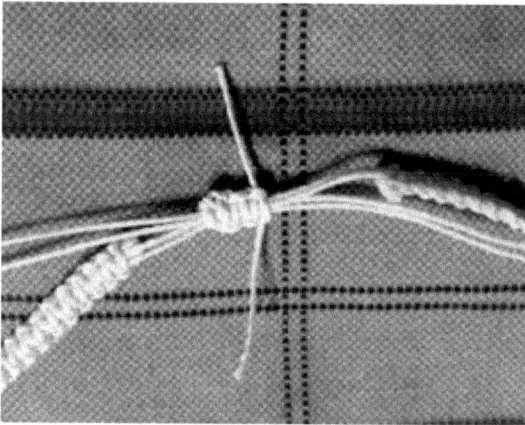

Step 12

Flip your necklace to have the bottom side up, then create a knot. Apply some glue to secure (as you had done earlier) and clip off the excess strands.

Pendant

Create a pendant! The beaded cord is attached to your finished micro-

Macramé centerpiece. Tropical lagoon colors combine to create the ebb and flow of this project. Anchoring things together is a lobster clasp. The finished length, stem to stern, is 10 inches. Cast off your cares and enjoy smooth sailing with this design!

Knots Used:

- Vertical Lark's Head Knot

- Flat Knot

- Half-Hitch Knot

Supplies:

- Blush C-Lon cord, 6 ft. cord (x4), 2 1/2 ft. cord (x1), 1 ft. cord (x2)

- 12mm Teal beads (x5)

- 8mm Tan beads (x8)

- Size 11 seed beads, teal (x14)

- 2.5mm Gold Crimp beads (x2)

- Size 6 seed beads, assorted teal and bronze (x133)

- 2mm Gold crimp beads (x2)

- Antique gold leaves, about 1mm (x3)

- Gold lobster clasp and jump ring

- Large gold crimp bead (U-shaped, might be labeled for leather cord) (x2)

- Glue - Beacon 527 multi-use

Instructions:

1. Place 4 cords through the ring at the top of an end crimp clasp. Fold the cords in half, for a total of 8 cords. Lay the cords in the crimp; glue and crimp shut. Turnover.

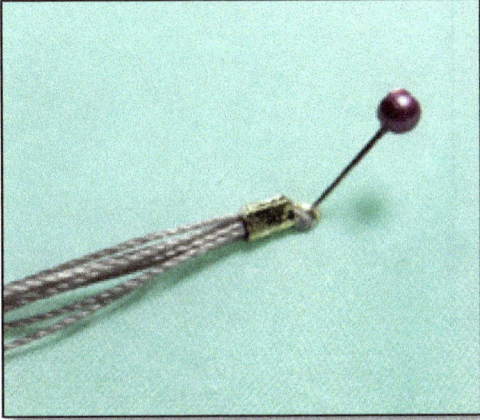

2. Tie a flat knot with outer 2 cords around all others.

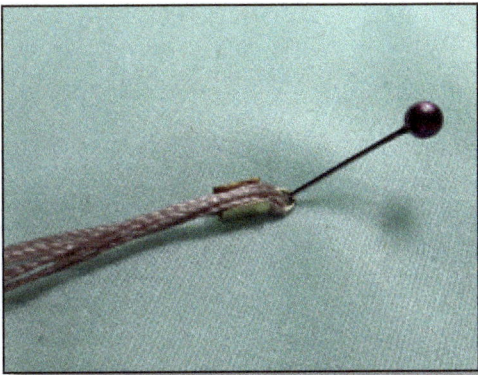

3. Separate 3-3-2. With the left 3: Find the left cord and tie 7 Vertical Lark's Head (VLH) knots around the other 2 cords.

4. With the center 3: Find the left cord and tie 3 VLH knots around the other 2 cords.

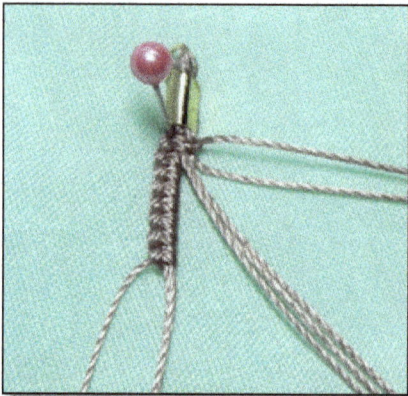

5. Place all 6 cords together. Bend the left section outwards, then take the left cord and tie a VLH knot around the other 5 cords. NOTE: tighten up each section as you attach them together.

6. With the left 3: Find the left cord and tie 5 VLH knots around the other 2 cords.

7. With the center 3: Thread a size 6 teal beads onto all 3 cords.

8. Place the left 6 cords together. Arc the left section outwards, then take the left cord and tie a VLH knot around the other 5 cords. (NOTE: tighten up each section as you attach them together).

9. With the left 3: Find the left cord and tie 7 VLH knots around the other 2 cords.

10. With the center 3: Find the left cord and tie 3 VLH knots around the other 2 cords.

11. Place these 6 cords together. Arc the left section outwards, then take the left cord and tie a VLH knot around the other 5 cords. (Remember to tighten things up). Set aside this section.

12. Using the right 2 cords: With the outer cord, tie 3 VLH knots onto the inner cord, then place a seed bead onto the outer cord. Tie 2 VLH knots, and then place a seed bead onto the outer cord. Tie 2 VLH knots with the outer cord, then put a seed bead onto the outer cord and tie 3 VLH knots.

13. Place all 8 cords together and find the left cord. Use it to tie a VLH knot around all others.

14. Repeat steps 2 to 11 to create the second section. Note: when starting the second section, move one of the longer cords to the outside to use as the knotting cord. You won't be able to tell that you snuck it over there.

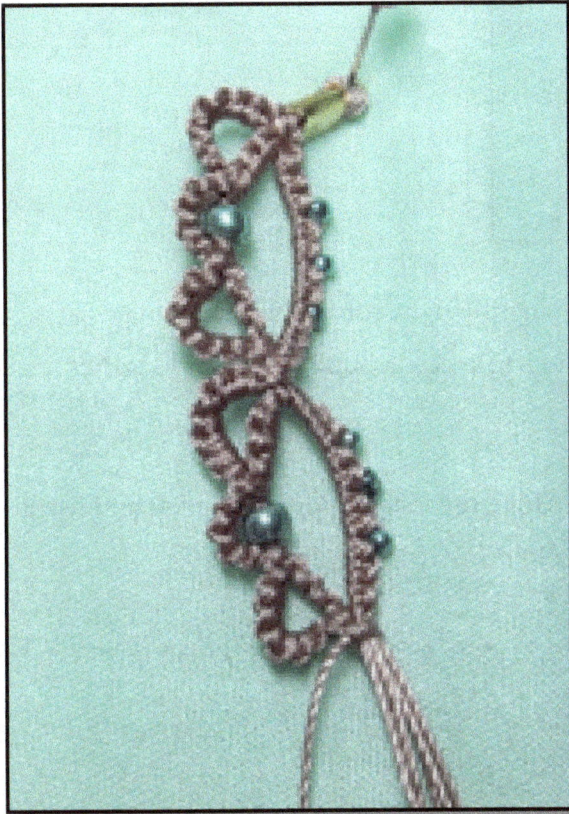

Center Section

15. Separate cords 2-2-3-1. Find the right cord and thread on a bronze size 6 bead, a 12mm teal bead, and another bronze size 6 bead. Set aside.

16. Find the right 3 cords. Using the right cord as the wrapping cord (WC), tie half hitch (HH) knots to create a bundle 3 ½ cm long. Set aside.

17. With the center 2 cords: Move the longest cord to the left and use it as the WC. Tie 9 VLH knots.

18. With left 2: Move the longer cord to the left to use as the WC. Tie 13 VLH knots.

19. Put the 4 left cords together and tie a VLH knot with the left cord.

Place 3 size 6 beads on the right 2 cords (teal, gold, and teal).

20. With the left 2: Tie 8 VLH knots. Put the 4 cords together and tie a VLH knot with the left cord.

21. With left 2, tie 13 VLH knots. With right 2, tie 9 VLH knots. Place the 4 cords together and tie a VLH knot with the left cord.

22. Put all 8 cords together and tie a VLH knot with the left cord. (End of Center Section)

23. Repeat steps 2 through 11 twice. Note: Tighten up the right 2 cords before working with them. If you start with the right cords here, this will lock things in place.

24. Turn the piece over and place the cords in the large crimp bead. Glue in place and crimp shut. Trim the ends.

Finishing

1. Place together the 2 ½ ft. cord and one of the 1 ft. cords, keeping the longer cord on the right. Thread them through the 2.5mm crimp bead, the lobster clasp, and back through the crimp bead. Crimp the crimp bead.

2. Bead as follows: (Note: when beading, be careful to keep the longer cord on the right at all times. If the cords get twisted inside the beads, it will skew the design).

3. Onto both cords; 1 dark teal, 1 frosted teal, 1 teal, 1 light copper, 1 dark copper, 1 light copper, 1 teal, 1 frosted teal, 1 dark teal followed by an 8mm tan bead. Repeat 3 times.

4. Place on cords 1 dark teal, 1 frosted teal, 1 teal, 1 light copper, 1 dark copper, and 1 light copper. Now separate the cords, with the longest cord to the right.

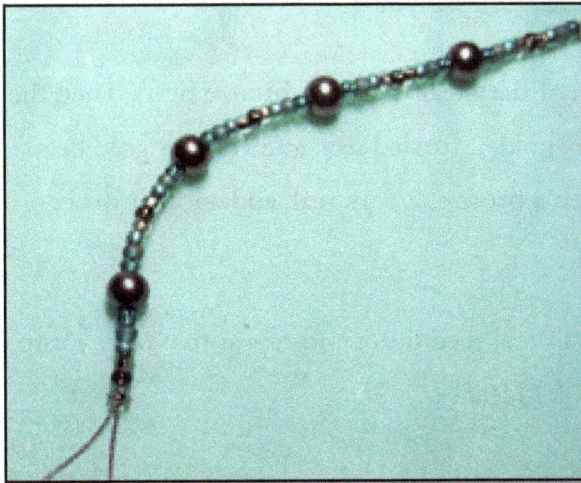

5. Onto the left cord, only place 1 teal, 1 frosted teal, 1 dark teal, 1 light copper, 1 dark copper, 1 light copper, then 1 dark teal, 1 frosted teal, and 1 teal. Now attach this cord to the pendant with a 2mm crimp bead.

6. Onto the right cord place: 1 dark teal, 1 gold, 1 bronze bead. Then the 12mm teal bead followed by gold, 2 frosted teal, and another gold bead. Thread on a 12mm teal, then a bronze, 2 dark teal, and another bronze bead.

7. Put on a gold leaf, a size 11 teal seed bead, and repeat that once more, then follow up with a third gold leaf.

8. Continue beading with a bronze, 2 dark teal, and another bronze bead followed by the 12mm teal bead. A size 6 gold, 2 frosted teal, and another gold bead go on next, then the last 12mm teal bead. Now 1 bronze, 1 gold, and 1 dark teal.

9. Tighten up the beading. Take the remaining 1 ft. cord and attach it to the right side of the pendant with a 2mm crimp bead.

10. Continue beading as shown – matching the first side (remember to keep the cords parallel inside the beads).

11. Thread both cords through the 2.5mm crimp bead, then through the jump ring and back through the crimp bead.

12. Tighten up the beading, then crimp the crimp bead. Glue and trim.

Macramé Spiral Earrings

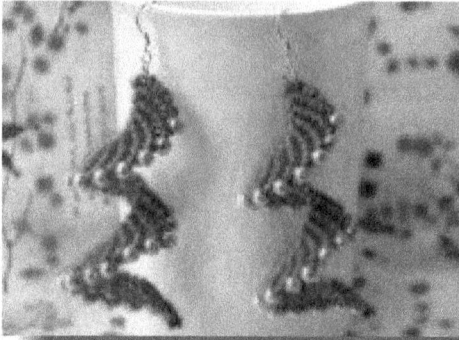

Materials:

- Lighter

- Earring hooks

- Jump rings

- 4mm light cyan glass pearl

- 1 mm nylon thread

Steps:

Cut three pieces of nylon thread at 100 cm. One of these would be the nylon thread, and the rest would both be the working threads. A crown knot should then be tied around the holding thread.

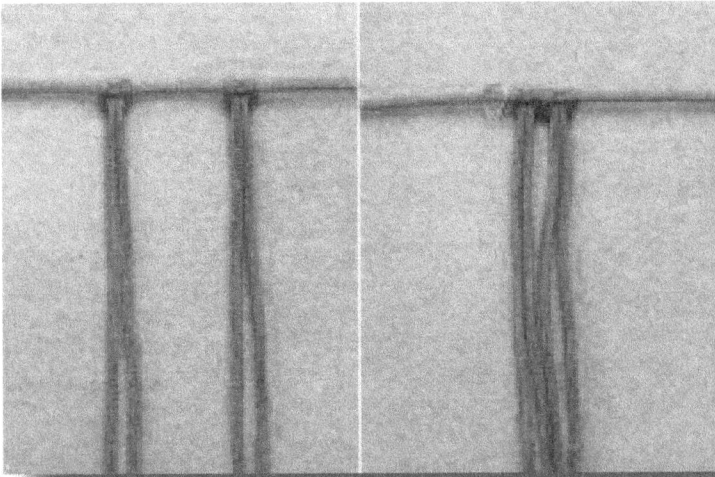

Check the left holding thread and make sure to add a jump ring there.

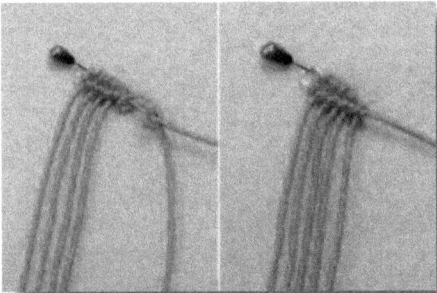

Over the four working threads, go ahead and place the left holding thread there. Use the four working threads to hold the thread and make a half hitch knot on the remaining thread.

Tie 4 half hitch knots on the leftmost thread and then slide a pearl onto the nylon thread. Secure with a half hitch knot.

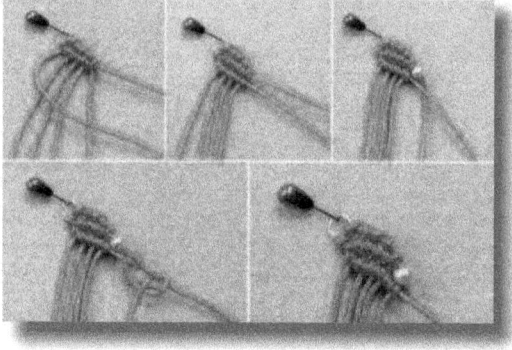

Repeat 25 times to create a perfect spiral.

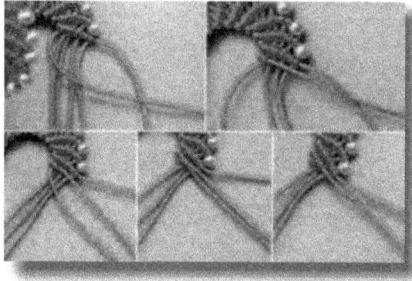

To fasten, get your holding thread again (the leftmost thread, in this case), and let it overlap the thread you are currently holding. Cut one holding thread after tying a half hitch knot.

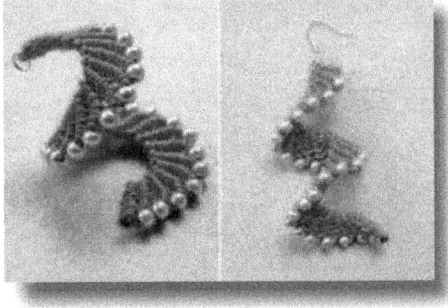

Tie two more half hitch knots and slide a pearl onto the rightmost thread. Make sure to use the thread in a half hitch again.

To finish, just cut some extra threads off and burn the ends with a lighter. Make sure to attach earring hooks, as well.

Summery Chevron Earrings

Materials:

- Ear wires

- Small chain

- Nylon/yarn (or any cord you want)

- Wire

- Pliers

- Scissors

- Hot glue gun

Steps:

Fold the cord into four and then tie a base/square knot as you hold the four lengths. Once you do this, you'll notice that you have eight pieces of cotton lengths with you. What you should do is separate them into two and tie a knot in each of those pairs before you start knotting with the square knot. It's like you're making a friendship bracelet!

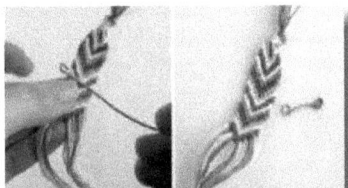

Use the wire to make two loops out of the thread and make sure the center and sides have the same width.

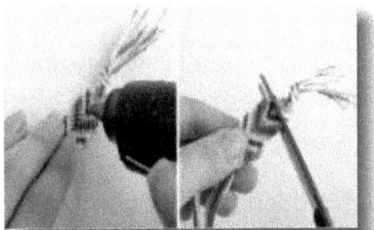

At the back of the bracelet, make use of hot glue to prevent knots from spooling.

Fold the bracelet around the wire shortly after putting some glue and letting it cool.

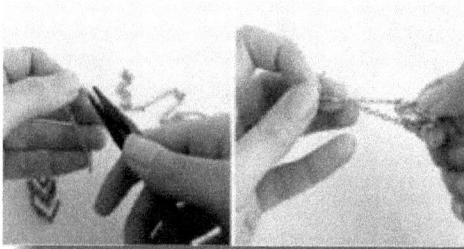

Use hot-glue so knots wouldn't come down again. Make sure to cut the excess thread.

Cut the chain to your desired length—or how you want the earrings to look like. Secure the ear wire as you find the middle of the chain.

Enjoy your new earrings!

Fringe Fun Earrings

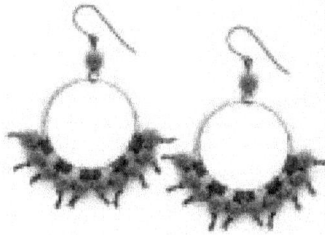

Materials:

- 56" of 4-ply Irish waxed linen cord

- 2 brass headpins

- 2 brass ear wires

- 2 hammered brass 33mm metal rings

- 22 glass 6mm rounds

- Round nose forceps

- Chain nose forceps

- Scissors

Steps:

Make eye pins out of the headpins by twisting the tip and making a

loophole, much the same as what's demonstrated as follows.

String a glass round to form a single loop and then set aside before cutting in half.

At the end of one cord, make a 3" fold and then go and knot around the brass ring.

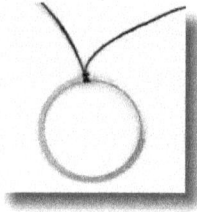

Make two half-hitch knots just around the ring.

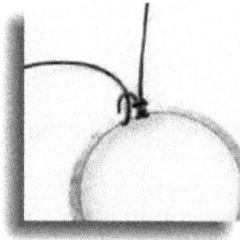

String a glass bead so that you could form an overhead knot. Trim until you reach 1/8" and make an overhand knot again. Trim once more to 1/8".

Climbing Vine Keychain

This pattern is a fun way to practice the Diagonal Double Half-Hitch knot. It works up quickly and is a fun piece to work in various colors. Just be sure to use enough beads on the fringe work to weigh the threads down.

Knots Used:

- Lark's Head

- Flat Knot

- Diagonal Double Half-Hitch

Supplies:

- Measure out 3 cords of Peridot C-Lon, 30" each

- 1 key ring

- 2 (5mm) beads

- 8 (plus extra for ends) pink seed beads

- 4 (plus extra for ends) gold seed beads

- 12 (plus extra for ends) green seed beads

- 8 (plus extra for ends) 3mm pearl beads (seed pearl beads will work also)

- Glue - Beacon 527 multi-use

Note: You can slightly vary the bead size. Just be sure that 2 cords will fit through the 2 main beads (the 5mm size beads).

Instructions:

1. Fold each cord in half and use a lark's head knot to attach it to the key ring. Secure onto your work surface with straight pins. You now have 6 cords to work with.

2. Separate cords into 3 and 3. Using the left 3 cords, tie 2 flat knots. Repeat with the right 3 cords.

3. Place all six cords together and think of them as numbered 1-6, left to right. Skip cord 1 and place a pink seed bead on cord 2. Skip cord 3 and place 2 gold seed beads on cord 4. Skip cord 5 and put 3 pink seed beads on cord 6.

4. Using cord 1 as your holding cord, tie a row of diagonal double half-hitch (DDHH) knots beginning on the left and ending on the right. Using cord 1 on the left, move it to the right as a holding cord and tie DDHH knots to the right.

5. Put all six cords together. Place 7 small beads on cord 1. Skip cord 2 and string your focal bead onto cords 3 and 4. Skip cord 5 and put 3 small beads on cord 6.

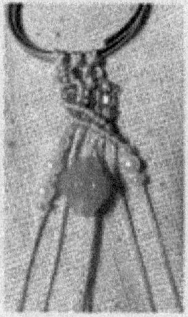

6. Use cord 6 as your holding cord and tie a row of DDHH knots from right to left. Repeat once more.

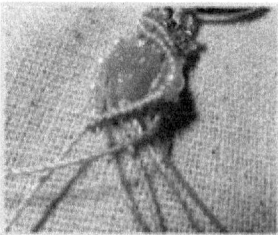

7. Repeat beading from step 3.

8. Repeat a row of diagonal double half-hitch knots from step 4 (left to right) twice.

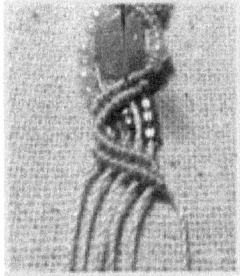

9. Place a bead as stated in step 5.

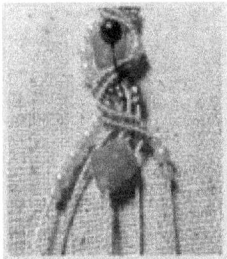

10. Repeat a row of DDHH knots as written in step 6 (right to left) twice.

11. Separate cords into 3 and 3. Tie 1 flat knot with the left 3 cords and 2 flat knots with the right 3 cords.

12. Separate cords into 1 – 4 – 1 and tie 1 flat knot with the center 4 cords only, letting cords 1 and 6 float.

13. Separate cords into 3 and 3. Tie 1 flat knot with each section.

14. Repeat step 12.

15. Bead ends with various size beads. Be sure there is enough weight to hold the ends downward. Tie an overhand knot with each cord and glue well. Let dry completely and trim cords.

Friendship Bracelet

Tools and Supplies

- Scissors

- Buttons (You can use a bead as well) Bamboo Cord or Hemp
  Twine

- Optional: Craft Glue

Method

Step 1

Cut out 2 pieces of cord that are around seven feet in length, which is
going to be a bit longer than required, but as we had mentioned earlier,

it's always good having a little extra instead of being insufficient. You can have them as the same color, but this pattern used two distinct colors.

Step 2

Next, measure approximately twelve inches and then double the cord up. This is going to give you two lengths of twelve inches and two, which are seventy-two inches. Create the overhand knot, which is going to be a loop for the closure of your button; therefore, you have to make sure that the button can fit through that loop.

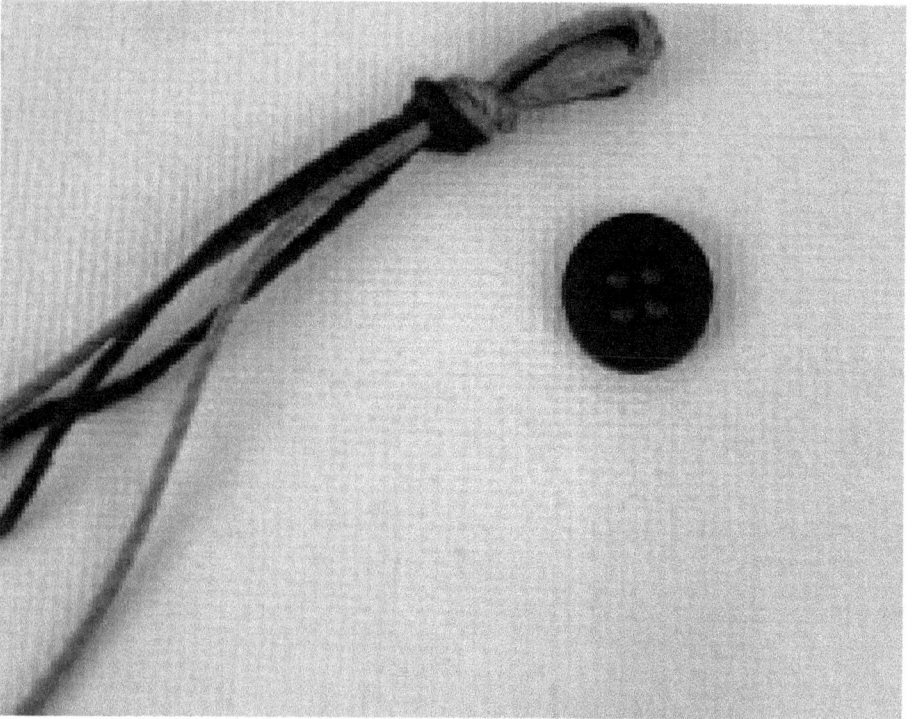

Step 3

Attach your bracelet to the project board or any work surface of choice.

Separate the strands to leave the two that are long on the sides and the two short ones at the center. Tie one of the strands that are long and knot it all around the two strands at the center. Using that exact cord, create another knot.

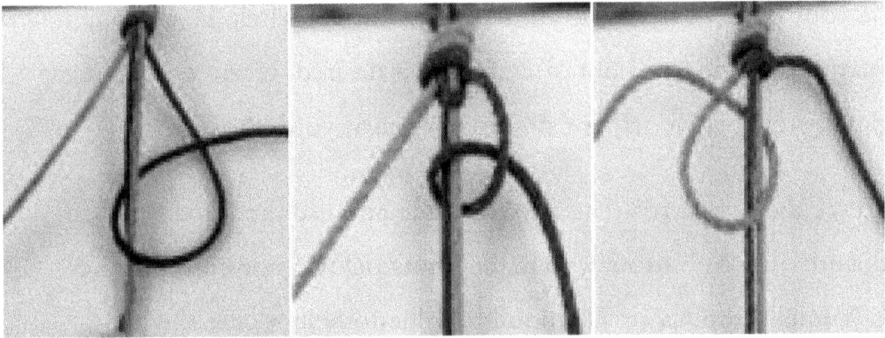

Step 4

Switch to the other cord and rework the 2 knots. Continue to alternate sides, creating 2 knots on either side.

Once you achieve your desired length (a woven length of approximately 6"), tie your bracelet off using an overhand knot. To help in securing it, you may apply a tiny amount of craft glue if desired. If you end up using the glue, you may clip off 2 of the tail ends near your knot.

Next, take the two cords that are remaining and use them for tying on the closure of your button. Create the knots below your button – then again, you may apply a small amount of glue to help secure the knot.

Macramé Hat Project

This Designer Hat features a rounded top with small triangles and an ornamental brim. Macramé design may be used as a basket.

I suggest that you simply use non-excessively versatile cord stock or that it won't hold its form. Within the example given, I used Bonnie Braid.

These instructions are written for a medium-size brim, 28 inches around. If you would like to form a smaller or larger hat, I've got provided you with cord measurements.

This is a simple project for beginners. Make sure to practice the ornamental knots mentioned below before you try and create this personalized hat if you're a new Macramé.

Supplies needed

- Material with 4 mm cord (114 yards)

- Planning Board and Pins

- Tissue glue

- Banding Test

Used Knots:

- Alternating Nodes in Square (ASK)

- Larks Tie Bottom

- Dual Third Coup (DHH)

- Overhand Node

Preparation

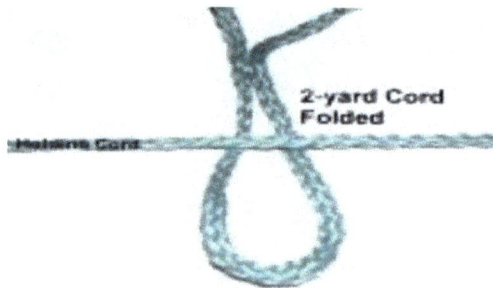

Step 1: Cut 56 strings, each 2 yards wide, for a medium-sized hat (28 inches across x 5 inches tall).

Take one 36 inches long carrying chain.

Cut 48 cords, 2 yards long, for a 24 "hat.

Cut 64 strings, 2.5 yards long, for a 32 "cap.

Just increase or decrease as required (2 cords per inch) for a Designer Hat above or below these sizes.

Make sure you sever a composite of 4 cords (36, 40, 44, etc.)

Prepare the ends by the film to stop unraveling.

Cord split in half. Attach the holding cord horizontally to the board and ensures it's taut.

Fold in half one among the 2-yard strings, and put it under the keeping string, so it lies within the center.

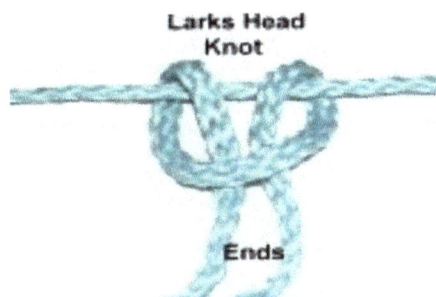

Larks Head Knot

Ends

Step 2: Taking the ends over the holding cord to finish the Larks Head Tie, head downwards.

Move them underneath the folded line. Stiffly tighten.

Step 3: Bind each end to a knot by putting the cord over-under the holding cord.

89

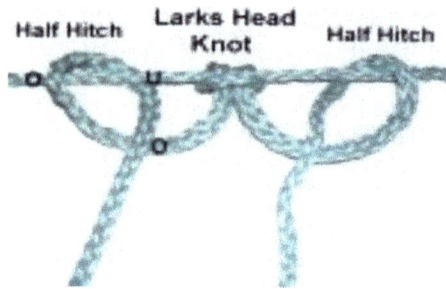

Half Hitch   Larks Head Knot   Half Hitch

This will give the chord you're coping with once you pull it back.

Step 4: Attach the remaining cords to the retaining string, replicate measures 1-3.

Job moves into the ends of the center.

Both directions should be equal in the number of cords.

Splitting Macramé Link

Building the sting

Step 1: Pick the primary 8 cords and mentally number them 1-8 (left to right) to make a brim for your Designer Hat.

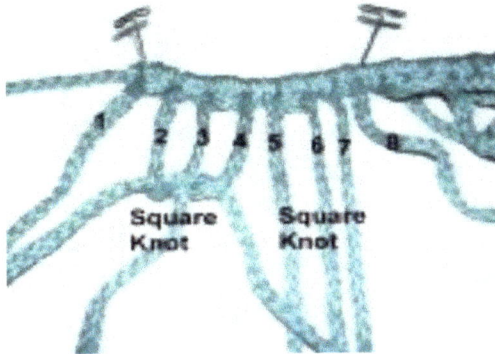

That of the triangle-shaped designs is created of 8 strings, so break them up now, before you continue.

SK: One Filler

Tie a 2-4 corded Square Tie. There's only one filler in there-cord 3. Firmly tighten it so it rests against the mounting knots.

Do likewise for 5-7 strings. Cord 6 is cord filler.

Step 2: Beneath the primary two, create another knot using cords 3-6 (two fillers — 4 and 5).

Firmly tie it until it lies on above knots

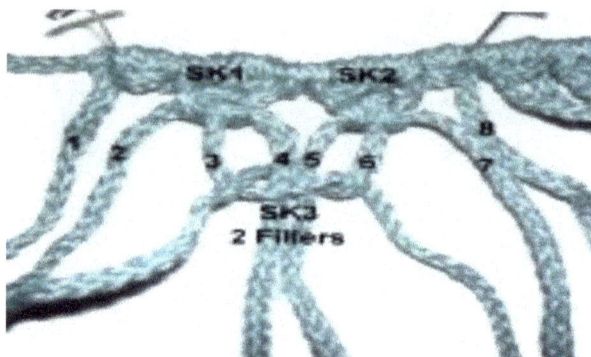

Step 3: Move cord 1 along the three knots on the left edge, forming a triangle. Lock it until it's taut, so it is a string to hold.

Connect Double Half Hitches to cords 2-4.

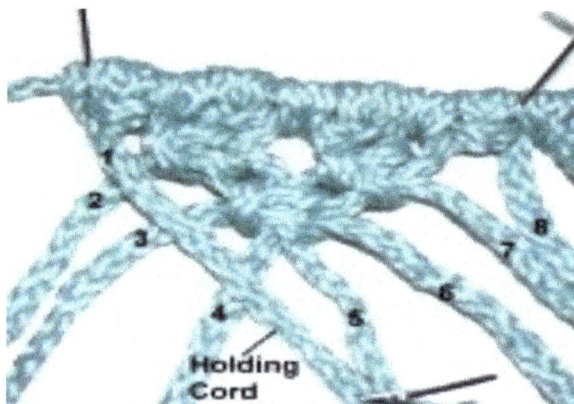

Step 4: Transfer and protect the cord 8 along the proper fringe of the Triangulum. Connect DHH 5-7 cords to that.

Be sure that you just don't add a holding cord 1, in order that the pattern is lopsided.

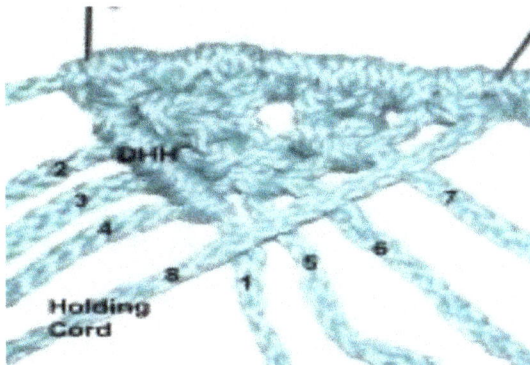

Step 5: Line the holding cables (1 and 8) and stretch out all the cables in order that you'll be able to easily see them.

Tie a knot with the 4, 8, 1, and 5 strings. The fillers are cords 8 and 1 firmly tie it, so the knot rests below the triangle level.

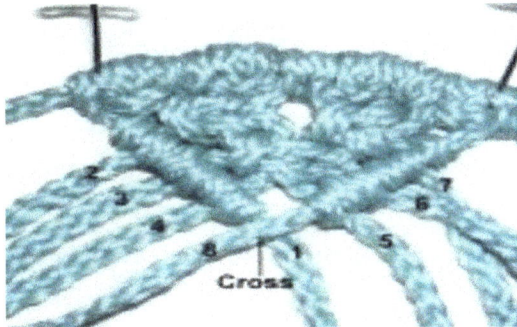

Step 6: Reverse steps 1-5, with the following 8 cords forming another triangle.

Attach an SK from the primary triangle with cords 6 and seven, and a couple of and three from the second.

Tighten it so that under each triangle it aligns with the SK.

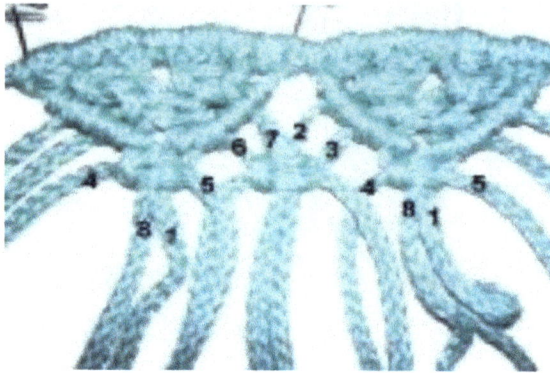

Step 7: Perform steps 1-6 together with other chord sections.

For your Designer Hat, once you hit the last triangle design, you wish to attach it to the primary one to make a circle.

Start by upside-down turning the brim of the Designer Hat pattern, because the front of the triangles is correct now within the cap.

Ensure to hide the sting, since the instructions are inverted.

You will see this within the picture below, which displays the triangles right where you're heading to function.

Triangles second and third

Tie an SK from the primary triangle with cords 2 and three, and 6 and seven from the second.

It is very much like what you probably did in phase 6, where the cords at each end of the brim pattern come from.

Locate the ends of the holding string used while mounting. Put one knot, add the adhesive, then put one over the previous.

Trim the ends to 2 centimeters, thread them under the mounting ties and add glue to stay them in the situation.

Mind the triangles are going to be at the sting, not the highest.

Designer Top Part Caps

Step 1: you'll tie rows of Alternating Square Knots with four cords per knot (2 working cords, 2 fillers) to create the highest portion.

Beginning at the place where the 2 ends were connected in step 7 is easiest, then traveling the whole route. Instead, rotate the subsequent set of cables.

Hold the sting in once you build your cap.

Mentally numbering four cords each set. The working cords are cords 1 and 4, with 2 and three as fillers.

Combine 3 and 4 with 1 and a pair of the next knot to alternate for the next row. Thus the new knot rests between the 2 above.

Step 2: Avoid binding Question when Designer Hat reaches a minimum of 7 inches from the underside fringe of the crown to the series of ties you use on.

Remember, you'll fold the brim, and you may still have some more rows to tie to the highest.

Step 3: Pick 12 cords from three ASK's.

Mentally label each set of 4 A, B, and C cords.

Move the four cords to the within of the Designer Hat from set B. Omit Four Strings.

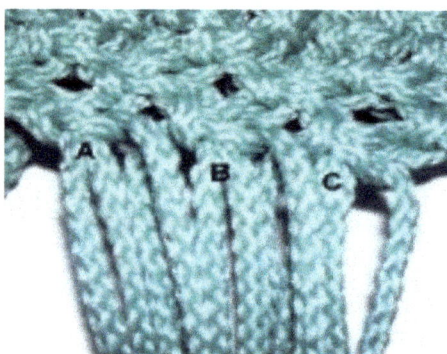

Step 4: Use cords 3 and 4 from set a (left), cords 1, and C (right) from set C.

Use these four cords to tie a good SK across the space left by the cords you pushed inside.

Stiffly tighten. This may make the hat top more rounded.

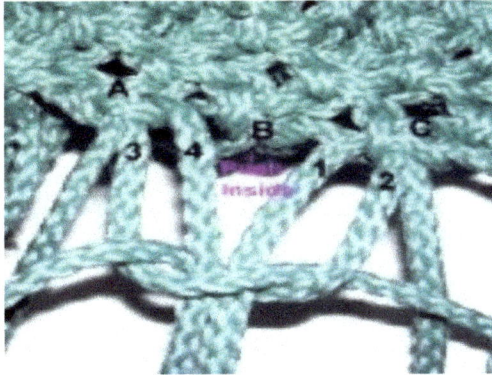

Step 5: Replicate stage 4 by moving it inwards, removing every other knot. This could sharpen the Designer Hat's rim.

Do steps 3 and 4 two more times until you have been all the way back? Push the remaining cords towards the within after you are through.

Step 6: Turn the hat around inside. Note that the within is that the front of the triangles and that they will be visible around the bottom edge once you are performing on this move.

Tie 2 very tight Overhand Knots using two cords at a time, from different knots.

If there are any big spaces, try crossing the gap by selecting cords from either side of it. Tie one knot, apply adhesive to the thread, then tie the knot next to the previous.

Having fixed the ties, cut the ends. If the cords have tape at the ends, you must take it off simply to be told which cords were used.

Have the glue dry and stop the surplus material in spite of everything the knots are tied.

Turn the Designer Hat's brims outwards, fold it at the constellation tip.

Silver Leather Bracelet

Tools and Supplies

- Two cord strands of round leather in 2 distinct sizes. For instance 1mm & 1.5mm. Each around eighty centimeters in length.

- One more round leather strand of the thinner (1mm) cord about 2m long.

- Thirty or so beads with a hole that is big enough to slide through the thinner leather.

- Optional: a bead with a huge hole

Method

Step 1

Fold the 2 eighty centimeter strands into half, then create a knot with a small loop. Try having the strands of thinner cord in between the thicker ones. Each of the four is going to be the "carry" cords.

Step 2

Take one thin carry cord and thread all your beads on it. Use a knot to secure it. Using a knot, secure the 2m strand over the "carry" cord. These are going to be the cords for working.

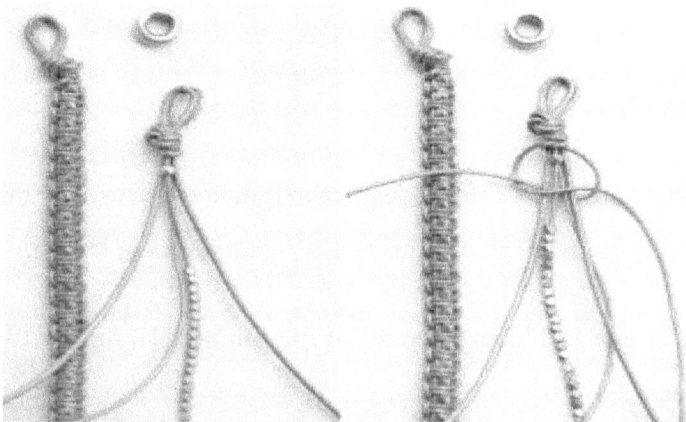

Step 3

Pull up the bead on one end and use your cords for working to create a square knot.

Pull the bead adjunct to it up, then use the exact square knot to secure it – decide whether it will be right or left facing, then go with it all the way.

Ensure that you gently pull every knot tight since the leather cord of 1mm is quite thin and is going to tear easily if pulled hard.

It is preferable that you secure the knot using your nails and fingers rather than yanking on your cords hard.

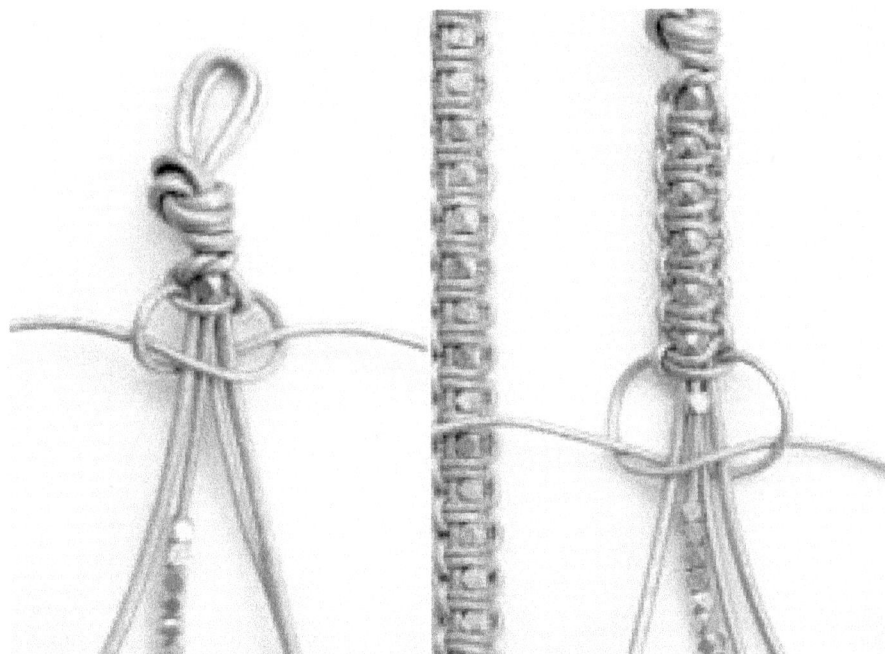

Step 4

Continue until you achieve your desired length and then form a huge knot using all the ends.

If desired, thread the bead via the huge hole and secure using a new knot.

Snip off the tips in either case and enjoy your new design.

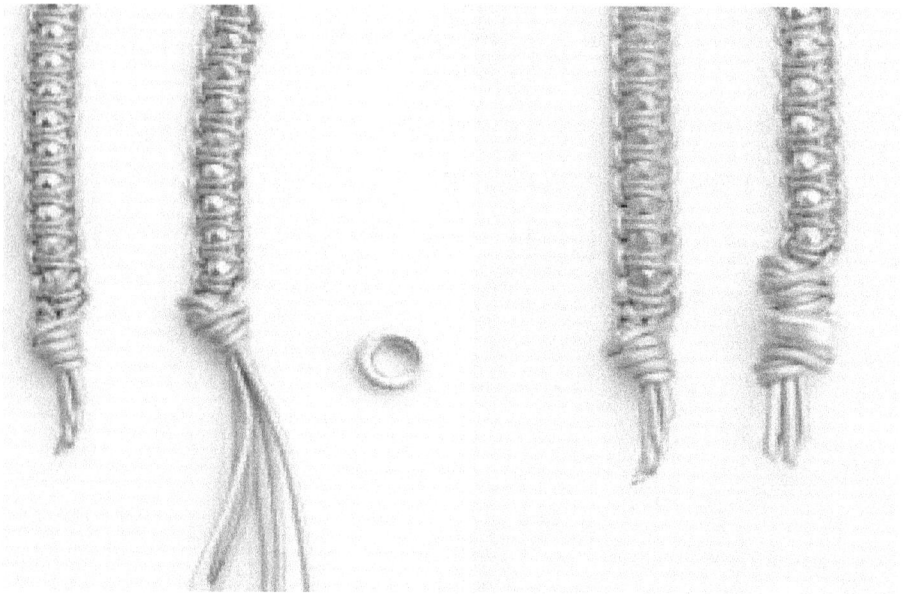

Stone Necklace

Tools and Supplies

- 4mm Chain – 24"-36" for each necklace, according to your preference Pliers (split ring pliers will be of great help) Embroidery Floss that is Brightly-colored Scissors

- Large Eye Needle

- Lobster Clasp

- 6mm Split Rings

- River Rock(s)

Method

Step 1

First, cut out four cords that are roughly eighteen inches each. This was more than enough for covering a stone measuring two to three inches. If using a smaller stone, then you are not going to require as much length, although it is always a good idea to have a length that is longer instead of one that is not sufficient.

Grab one strand on a split ring and a cord (you may simply use the typical jump ring, although this makes sure it doesn't, later on, slip off the chain). Place your ring in the middle of your strand, then tie it all around the middle points of the remaining three cords. This is going to form a central ring having eight strands (nine inches in length) that are comprehensively knotted in the middle.

Pair 2 cords that are next to one another next. Join the 2 cords using the overhand knot at around half an inch from the mid-ring in every cord pair.

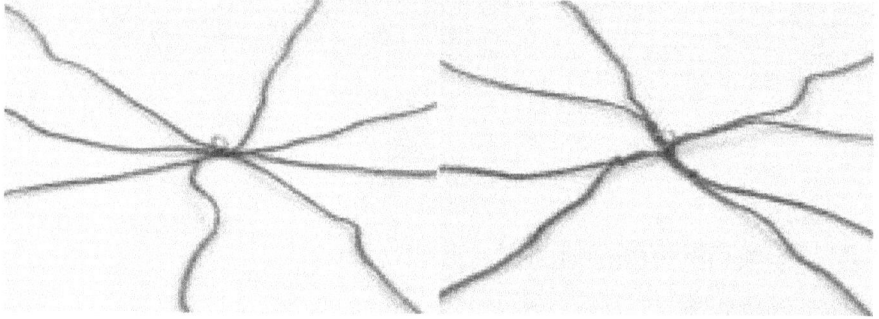

Step 2

Separate the cord pairs, then pair them once again using the adjunct cords at approximately half an inch from the original knot set. You are going to keep separating and alternating the pairs, thus forming knots near the final knot set.

Note: You will have to position your knots near the mid-ring and nearer one another if the stone you are using is small. We are forming some type of "net" for holding the stone, and the farness between your knots is going to establish the largeness of the holes.

Step 3

Smaller stones are going to need smaller holes. To get an ideal distance, you might require to test using your stones. As you work, try to slip the stone you will be using inside your net to find out if it's a suitable fit.

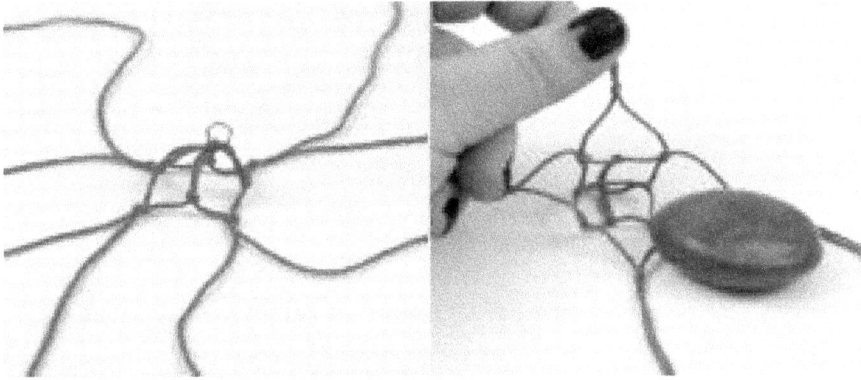

Step 4

Once you have made a net that is big enough for holding your stone, slip the stone inside, then tightly wrap it around the stone. To tighten it, divide your cords into two sections, then tie them to one another in the same way as to how a shoe is tied. To make it tighter around your stone, create a double knot. To give it a nice beautiful finish, create the overhand knot you're your double knot.

Make a tassel by trimming the ends off, and there you have it; your macramé stone necklace.

If you want, you may do some easy weaving to brighten your chain up to match the stone pendant. Cut out a stand of embroidery floss that is six to eight inches longer than the chain you are using. On one tip of your chain, create a knot, then string your floss onto a needle with a large eye. Wrap your floss in and out through your chain, securing it with a knot on the remaining end of your chain.

Step 5

String the pendant, then link a ring on one chain end, then to complete the necklace, attach one ring and lobster clasp on the remaining end.

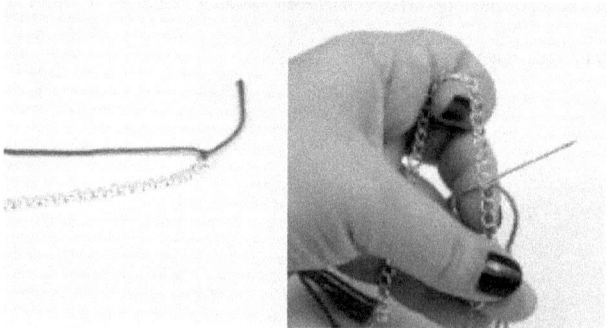

106

Macramé Tassel Earring

The most effective method to make macramé tassel earrings.

We're currently getting into one of my preferred macramé projects – hoops! All the more explicitly, tassel hoops.

In case you're hoping to get some motivation and ideas for your next macramé project, look no further, as macramé earrings are an incredible apprentice amicable project you can rapidly begin with.

Macramé earrings are easy to make and are ideal for any event. You can wear them as a fashion statement, blending and coordinating with different accessories. It is a great method to show your exceptional style and artistry – I appreciate making macramé earrings, therefore.

For this macramé project, you will spend around 45 min – 1 hour to make them. You will utilize just two knots for this project – a twofold half knot tie an overhand tie. You will no doubt need to get yourself some macramé string and a couple of band earrings for this project.

If earrings interest you, be certain you give this macramé DIY project a go!

Materials Needed:

- 3mm Cotton Cord

- Weaving String

- Earrings

- Length of Cotton Cord:

- 6 x (3" –5") threads (for one hoop)

- • Length of Embroidery String:

- 1 x 22" (for one earring)

Instructions

Step 1: To begin, cut three pieces of your cotton macramé cord. A piece should be 12-inch and the other two pieces, 6-inch. Fold the 12-inch cord piece into half, bringing the loop to the top. Fold one of the 6-inch cord piece into half, tucking the loop beneath the top of the 12-inch piece, from right to left.

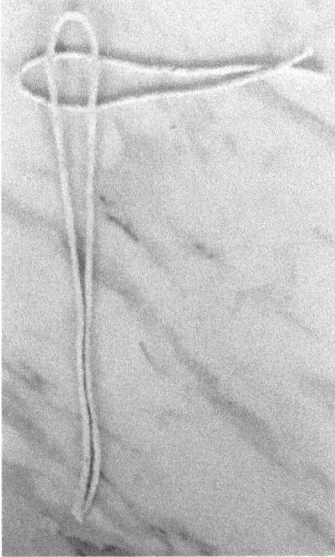

Step 2: Fold the second 6-inch cord into half and tuck this loop up across the first 6-inch cord loop, from left to right.

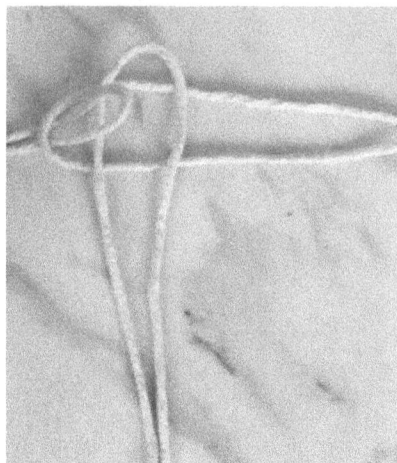

Step 3: Pull the second 6-inch cord through the middle of the 12-inch cord, inserting the ends of the first 6-inch cord across this loop.

Pull both sides of the cords to tighten the knot.

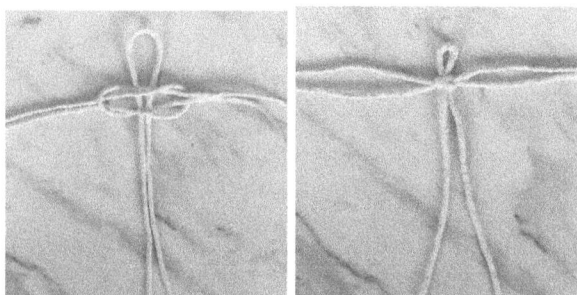

Step 4: Repeat the steps of adding extra two 6-inch loops and tying this knot, but this time, alternate the sides where the first loop was inserted – insert the first loop beneath the middle cord from the left while the

second should be from the right. Then start again, this time from the right. Do this continuously until there are ten knots.

Trim the ends into a leaf shape.

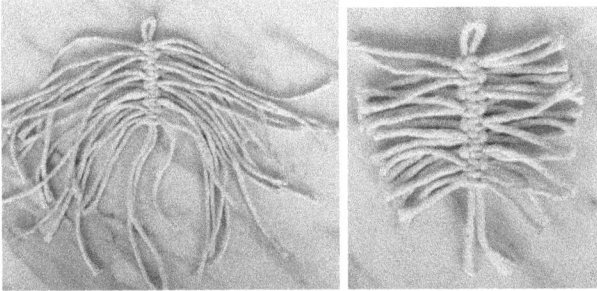

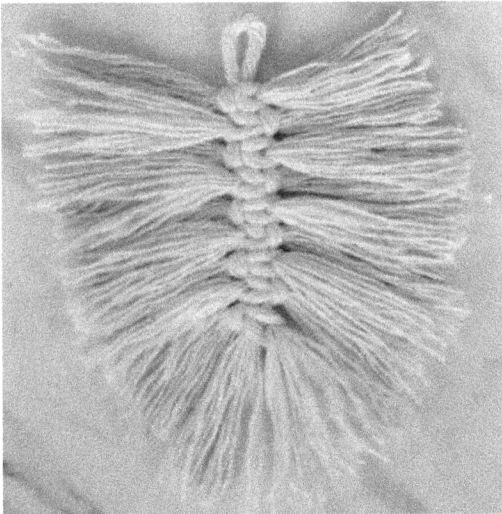

Step 5: Fray and separate the strands of the cords using your fingers and the wire comb. Brush gently using the comb.

Step 6: Trim again to make a leaf shape then brush with a comb. Add the jump ring to the top loop of the macramé cord.

Double Coin Knot Cuff

Materials:

- 9 m (10 yds.) 2 mm leather cord

- 3 x 9 mm internal dimension end caps magnetic fastening

Steps:

1. Cut the leather cord into three equal pieces, 3 m (3 1/3 yd.) long. Referring to Chinese Knots: Double Coin Knot, tie a double coin knot using all three strands starting in your left hand with a clockwise loop and pulling down the working end (right-hand tail) over the thread. Complete

the knot and make it tight so that the top loop is relatively wide and all three strands are smooth and neatly aligned.

2. Make a second double coin knot, this time starting with a loop in your right hand, bringing the working end (left-hand tail) down through the loop, around the other tail, and doubling back to create the second knot.

3. Firm the second knot, adjust the position so that the previous knot is fairly close but does not overlap. Make sure none of the cords are twisted and that they all lie flat inside the knot.

4. Continue to tie double coin knots one by one, and swap the starting position from side to side each time.

5. Analyze the length of the cuff until you've made six knots. If required, adjust the distance between each knot to allow for the fastening.

Overlap the cords after the final knot to create a circle. Either tie the cords together or stitch them across to hold the cord flat, depending on the style of your end cap (see Finishing Techniques). Trim the ends and use epoxy resin glue to hold them into the end caps.

Fish Bone Macramé Bracelet

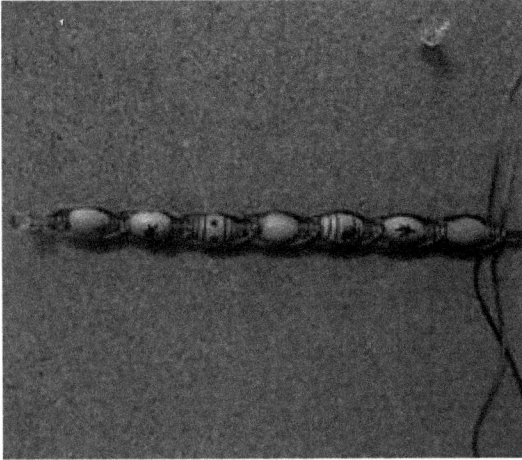

Materials

15cm Blue cord

Beads/buttons to fit

Red cord

A Lighter

A needle or point of a pair of scissors

Instructions

Step 1. Fold the shorter blue cord in half and lay it in front of you.

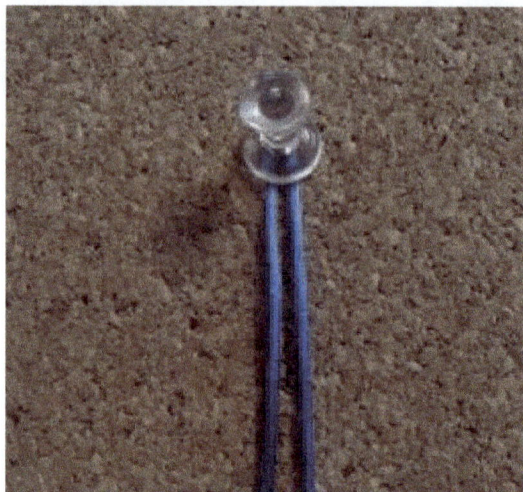

Step 2. Fold the long blue cord in half, and tie one square knot around the shorter cord.

This knot should be positioned so that the loop created is a tight fit for the bead/button to fit through.

Step 3. Use the red cord to tie a square knot underneath the bead.

Step 4. Place a thread on the first bead.

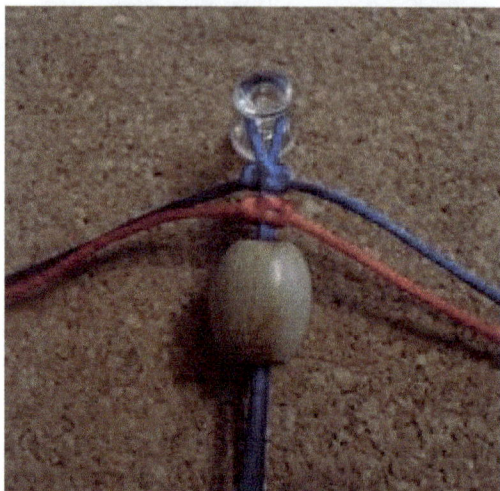

Step 5. Carry the blue cords over the red and tie a square knot underneath the bead.

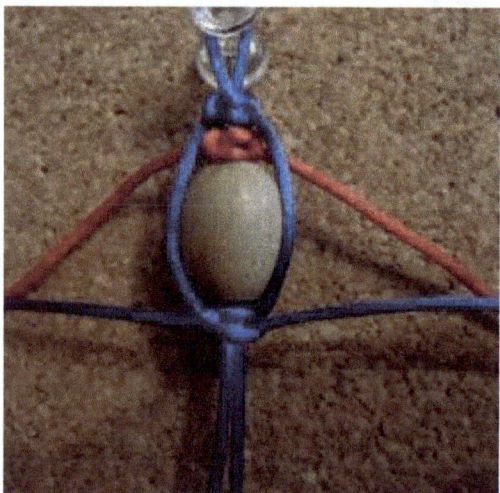

Step 6. Carry the red cords over and tie a square knot underneath the blue knot.

118

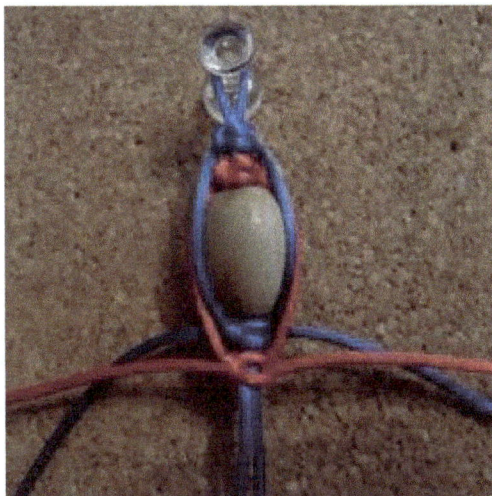

Step 7. Place a thread on a second bead.

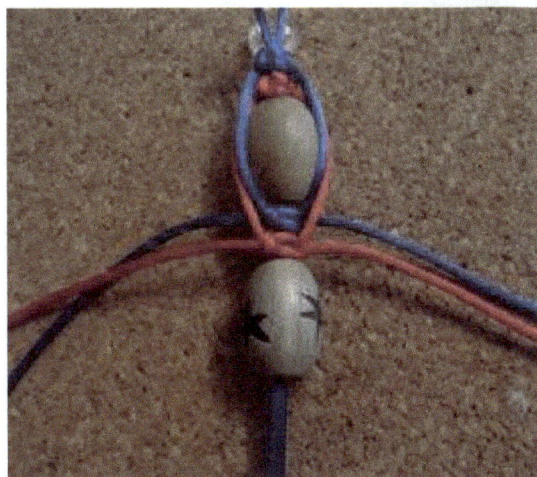

Step 8. Repeat Step 5 and Step 6.

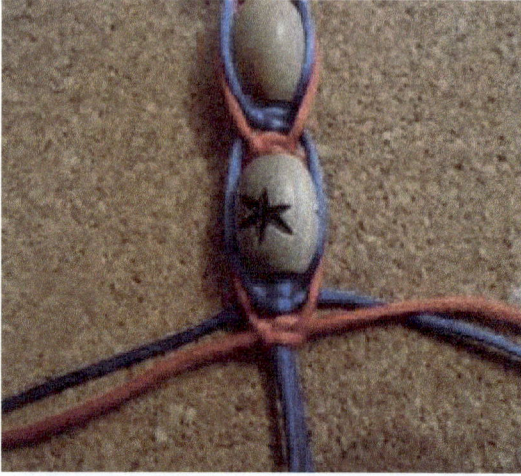

Step 9. Continue in this way until all the beads have been added.

Step 10. Leave a 3 mm tail cut off the remaining knotting cord on one side. Use the lighter to melt the ends and stick them to the back of the knots.

Take care while handling the melting cord as it gets very hot and can stick to your skin and burn. Again, use a needle or point of a pair of scissors to press down the cord.

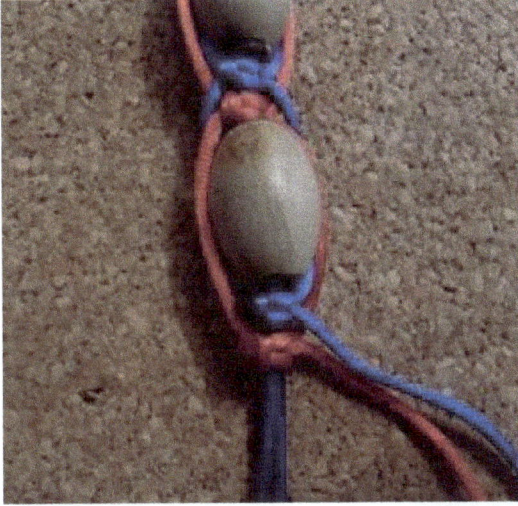

Step 11. Repeat Step 10 with the remaining cords.

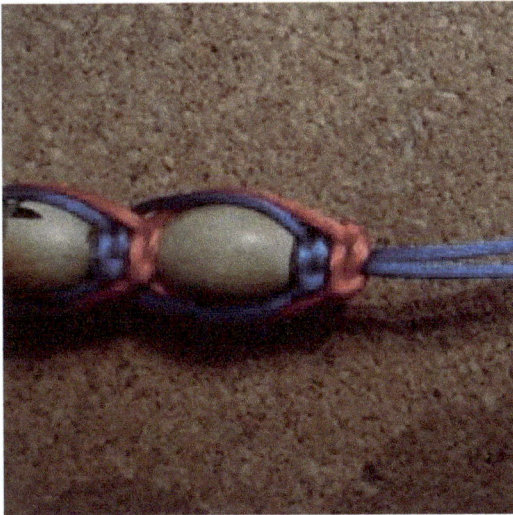

Step 12. Place a thread on the disk bead/button. Leave a 3 mm gap between the final knot and the bead and tie an overhand knot. Cut off any excess cord and melt the ends to prevent fraying.

Cross Choker

Step 1 - Fold over the first 1.5 inches if the shorter length of rattail cord. This will be used to create a loop as part of the bracelets fastening.

Step 2 - Fold the longer length of cord in half. Place the center point underneath the shorter cord and tie one square knot. These will be your knotting cords. This knot needs to be positioned so that it creates a loop in the end of the shorter cord that the disk bead can fit through with some pressure. If the bead slides through too easily there is a possibility that the bracelet could come unfastened.

Step 3 - Tie a further five square knots.

Pull each knot tight as these are holding the two lengths of cord together.

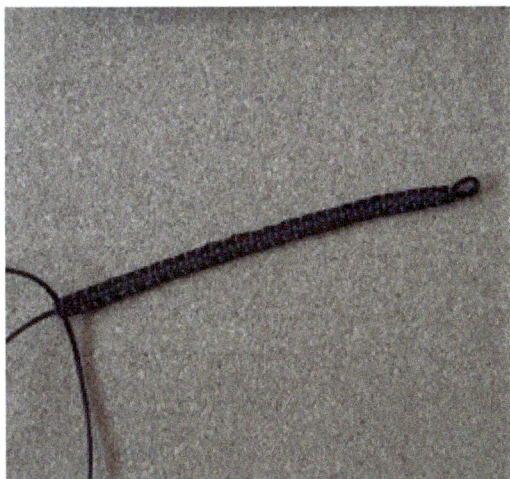

Step 4 - Continue tying square knots until you have a Sennett 5.5 inches long.

Step 5 - Thread one silver foil bead on to the central cord.

Step 6 - Bring the knotting cords around the bead and tie one square knot.

Step 7 - Now thread on one cross charm and push it up to the last

square knot. Because of the hole positioning the cross will not lay flat

Step 8 - Tie another square knot around the cross top.

Step 9 - Continue with steps 5 - 8 until all the beads and crosses have been added.

Step 10 - Now tie another Sennett of square knots 5.5 inches long.

Step 11 - Leaving a 3mm tail cut of the excess knotting cords. Using the lighter gently melt the ends and press them on to the square knots. Care needs to be taken with this step as the melted cord can get very hot and stick to skin and burn. It is best to use a needle or scissor point to press down the cord.

Step 12 - Thread the disk bead (or button) on to the remaining cord.

Step 13 - Leaving a 3mm gap tie an overhand knot to secure the bead.

Step 14 - Cut of the excess cord and heat the ends gently with the lighter to seal and prevent fraying.

Dyed Macramé Necklace 2

Follow the instructions below to make one for yourself.

What you will need

- Leather lace (long enough to tie around your head)
- Cotton string
- Fabric dye

Instructions

Step 1: Cut a 3 ft long, 8 pieces of cotton string

Step 2: Each string should be folded into half, then tie it to the leather lace using lark's head knot. Tape the untied leather across a table to prevent the top of your necklace from moving around.

Step 3: Make a square knot in sets of four with the 16 strings hanging down. To make a square knot, the first four strings on the left should be taken across string 1, then over string 2 and 3, beneath string 4. Then take string 4 and wrap it beneath string 1 on the right. Continue right under string 2 and 3 then over string 1 on the left.

Step 4: From the last activity in step 3, tighten to the top. Then take string 1 (now on the left) over string 2 and 3, beneath string 4. Take string 4 and wrap it beneath string 1 on the left. Continue this beneath

2 and 3, branching over string 1 on the right side. Tighten to the top as earlier done.

Step 5: For the knots on the top, alternating square knots were used. A square knot for strings 1-4, 5-8, 9-12, 13-16 for row one, strings 3-6 and 11-14 for row two, strings 1-4, 5-8, 9-12,13-16 for row three, strings 3-6 7-10, 11-14 for row four, strings 5-8 and 9-12 for row five, and strings 7-10 for row six.

Then a few random knots were tied on the remaining strings hanging and the bottom trimmed.

Step 6: The leather lace should be tied such that your head fits in it when it is worn.

Step 7: For the dye, RIT box dye was used. Just follow the RIT stovetop instructions on how to heat the water and dye.

Step 8: Dip the necklace into the water as high as you want the dye to go up the necklace, then pull it out just a bit, tying it to the handle of the pot to soak for sometime. Continue pulling it up for every 5 -10 minutes for a slight ombre look to be formed.

Rinse it out and allow it to dry.

Macramé Rings

Tools and Supplies

A round object that is the exact size as your finger – if you use multiple colors/thicker yarn, it helps to use something a bit larger, or else the ring might not fit.

- Glue
- Scissors
- Yarn – around 1.2m will do

Method

Step1

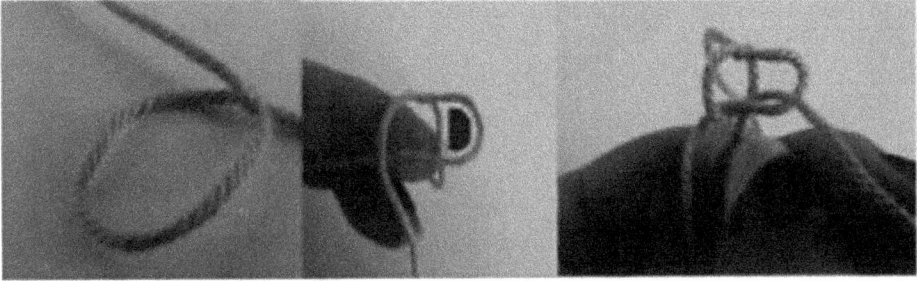

Start by folding your strand of yarn into equal halves then place it around your round object. Use the 2 tails to create a simple knot. This would be the perfect time to confirm that your strands are of equal lengths. Secure your initial knot by creating another knot. You may now remove your ring from your round object and begin to macramé.

Step 2

Begin by crossing the strand on the right side over the strand at the center then up. Make sure to fasten it by pulling tightly complete the

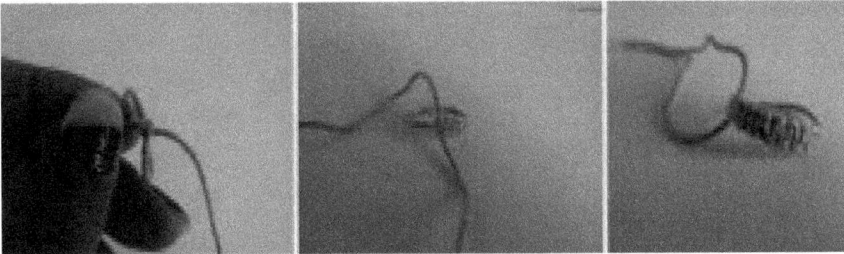

first knot.

Step 3

This step is basically similar but mirrored. Begin by crossing the strand on the left side over the strand at the center; allow the strand on the right side to pass below the strand at the center then up again. Carry on creating the 2 knots until you are nearly done with the ring.

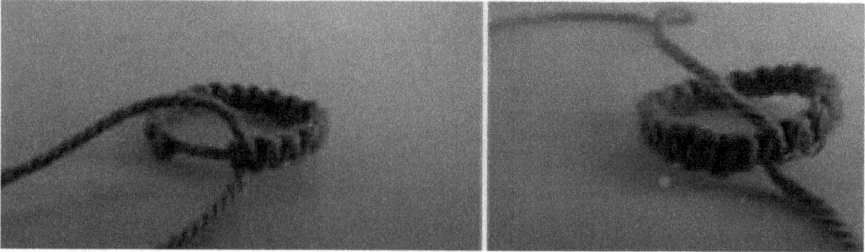

Step 4

Once you create the final macrame knot, be sure to tighten it by pulling then create a simple knot at the top of your ring.

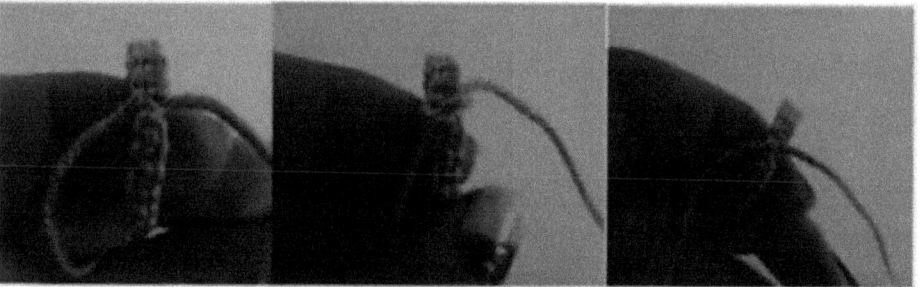

Step 5

Apply some glue then trim the tips. Ensure that you cover the ends in glue, as well to have a smooth finished ring.

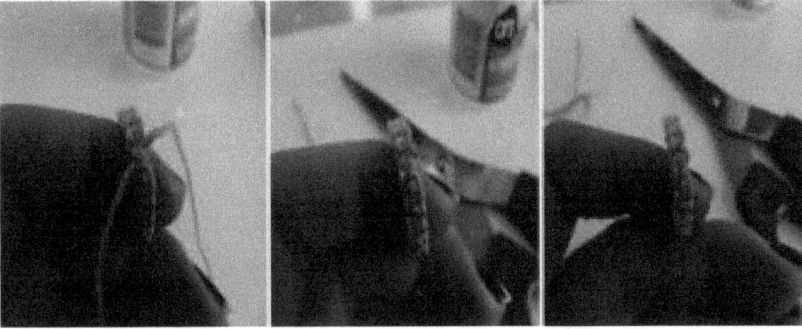

Necklace

A leather necklace has that rustic and earthy feel. Now, if you want to add some edge to an already beautiful thing, you could try Macramé and go and knot the thread!

What you need:

- Pliers
- Scissors
- Chain
- Crimp ends
- Jumprings
- Clasp
- 7 silver beads
- 5 meters of leather cord

Instructions:

Cut leather into a meter each and make 4 parts, then make a four-strand braid out of it.

Make use of the square knot to secure the loops. Copy on the left side of the cord.

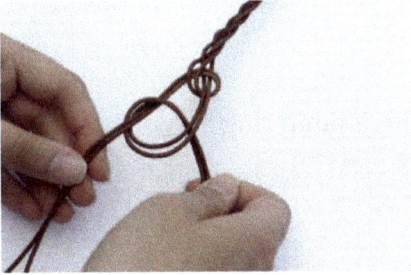

Add beads after you have done the first two knots. Hold it as you hold the right string. Create an empty knot, loop, and add some beads again.

Secure both ends of the cord using the crimp end. You could also use glue to keep it all the more secure.

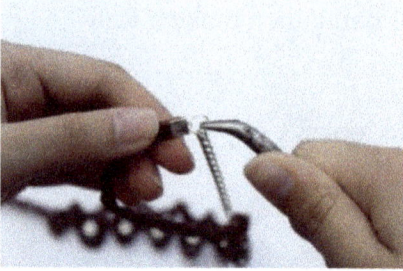

Attach a piece of the chain at the end with a jump ring so your necklace could be ready.

Enjoy your new necklace!

Macramé Gem Necklace

This one has that enchanting, beautiful feel! Aside from knots, it makes use of gemstones that could really spruce up your look! Surely, it's one necklace you'd love to wear over and over again!

What you need:

- Your choice of gemstones
- Beads
- Crocheted or waxed cotton
- Water
- Glue

Instructions:

Get four equal lengths of cotton—this depends on how long you want the necklace to be.

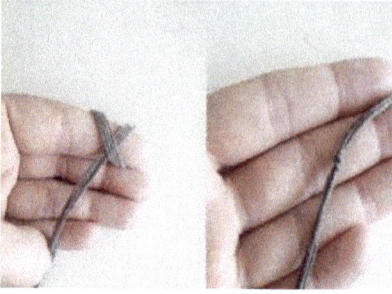

Tie a base knot as you hold the four cotton lengths. Once you do this, you'd notice that you'd have eight pieces of cotton lengths with you. What you should do is separate them into twos, and tie a knot in each of those pairs before you start knotting with the square knot.

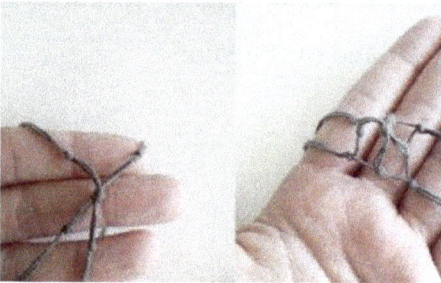

Tie individual strands of the cotton to the length next to it. Make sure you see some depth before stringing any gemstones along, and make sure to knot before and after adding the gemstones to keep them secure.

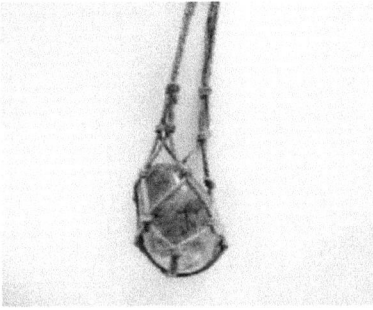

Take four of the strands in your hand and tie a knot on the top side of the bag. Tie strands until you reach the length and look you want. Knot the ends to avoid spooling, and use water with glue to keep it more secure.

Endless Falls Macramé Bracelet

Materials:

- 60cm length of 2mm black waxed cotton cord

- 40-inch length of red waxed cotton cord

- 1 8-10mm flat bead

Tools List

- Macramé board and Pins (optional)

- Scissors

- Ruler

- PVA glue

Steps:

Step 1 - Fold the black cord in half and lay it in front of you or pin it to your macramé board.

Step 2 - Fold the red cord I half and place the halfway point underneath the black cords.

Step 3 - Cross the red cords over the front of the black. It does not matter which cord is on top, but ensure that it is the same in each knot or the pattern will not form correctly.

Step 4 - Pick up the black cords and thread them through the loop formed by the red cords and between the two black cords.

Step 5 - Tighten the knot by pulling the black cords downwards. Position the knot approximately 1cm below the black cord ends, creating a loop. This loop is part of the bracelet clasp, so it needs to be tightened well for the bead to pass.

Step 6 - Cross the red cords over the front of the black cords.

Step 7 - Pick up the black cords and thread them through the loop formed by the red cords and between the two black cords.

Step 8 - Pull the black cords downwards to tighten the knot until it rests beneath the first knot.

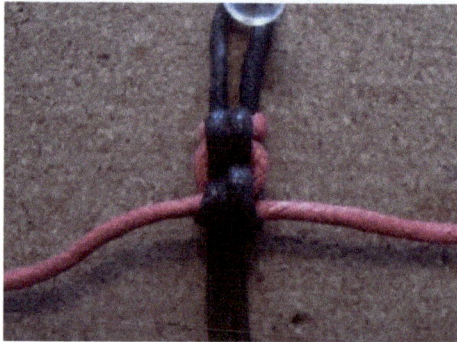

Step 9 - Repeat steps 6-8 until the bracelet measures 7.5 inches long. Holding all four cords at the cross over point with one hand while threading the black cords with the other is a good technique for tying this type of knot.

Step 10 - Now tie one square knot using the red cords and pull the knot tight

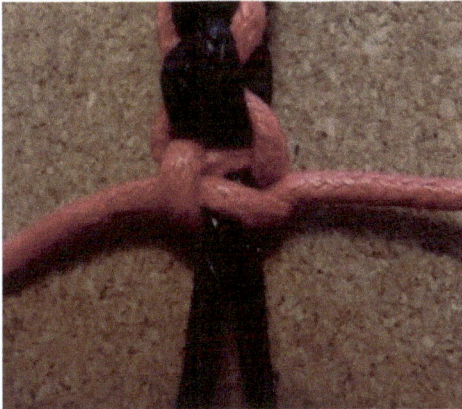

Step 11 - Cut off the excess red cords and one of the lengths of the black cord.

Step 12 - Cover the cut cord ends and the surrounding area in PVA glue and leave until dry.

Step 13 - Thread the flat bead onto the remaining black cord. Leaving a 3mm gap, tie an overhand knot to secure the bead.

Step 14 - Cut off the remaining cord leaving a short end. The cord end can be dipped in PVA if desired to stop it from fraying.

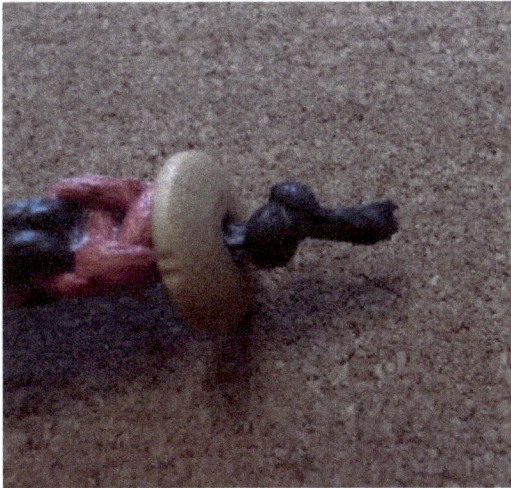

Snake Knot Tie Backs

Materials:

- 5 m (5 1/2 yd.) 3 mm teal elastic cord

- Swarovski Elements: XILION beads 5328, 4 mm pacific opal and chrysolite opal, 54 each

- Seed beads 11 (2.2 mm) blue marbled aqua and silver-lined crystal

- Nylon beading thread

- Size 10 beading needle

- Two end caps with 3 x 9 mm internal dimension

- Epoxy resin adhesive

Steps:

1. Cut a 45 cm (18 in) length of Referring to Knotted Braids: Snake Knot, work the braid on your snake knot.

2. Tie a knot to a beading thread at the end of a nylon length (or equivalent color), and thread 10 beading needle. Bend the braid from the end about 5 cm (2 in), so you can see the pattern of the cord between the loops on one side. Place the needle of a tapestry between the two straight braid lengths you can see.

3. Move the needle of the tapestry through the braid to escape between the loops on the other side. Leave the needle in place for the tapestry; this is the direction the finer threaded needle takes through the braid.

4. Hold the nylon thread between two lateral loops above the needle. Pick an aqua seed bead, a pacific opal XILION, an aqua seed bead, a silver seed bead, a chrysolite opal XILION, a silver seed bead, an aqua seed bead, a pacific opal XILION, and an aqua seed bead.

5. Place the beads through the braid at an angle, then take the beading needle back alongside the tapestry needle. Remove all needles simultaneously.

6. Pull the thread taut over the braid to protect the beads. Between the next loops thread the tapestry needle again through the braid in order to attach another line of beads. This time the XILIONS order is inverted, adding two opal chrysolite and one opal pacific.

7. Repeat to add bead lines, stopping from the end of the braid about 5 cm (2 in) apart. Sew firmly in ends of thread.

8. Cut the cord to the same length, leaving the tails approximately 2 cm (3/4 in) long. Mix a bit of epoxy resin adhesive and put a cocktail stick within one end cap. Place two of the cord ends in the end cap and force the remaining cord in place using a cocktail stick (or awl). At the other end, repeat to add an end cap, and leave to dry.

Pandora Bracelet

Tools and Supplies

- Fabric glue (clear when dry) Project board

- Tape

- Pins

- Pandora beads

- 2mm of cord material (this pattern used Satin)

Method

Step 1

Cut out two cords that are not less than 72" in length to make a bracelet that is 8". To avoid unraveling, apply glue to the tips.

Horizontally align your cords, then secure them close to the middle. Mark the middle point using a sheet of tape. Thread your first bead through the two cords to have it resting over the tape.

Step 2

Working at the same time, create a loop that is counterclockwise using the 2 cords.

Pro tip:

The best way to secure satin and other cords that are delicate are by leaning pins over them. When you place the pins through your material, it is going to destroy the frail fibers.

Center

Counter-
Clockwise

Step 3

Fold the end that is free to create a bight. Bring it under-over through your loop.

To make the initial loop tight, yank the bight. As you do that, get rid of the slack from the bead segment so that the loop you tightened is against the bead. Pull carefully as this is a crucial step in the design.

Pass Bight
Through Loop

Pull Bight
To Tighten
First Loop

Step 4

Pass the end that is free below your bead by rotating clockwise. Ensure that your knot is not twisted. It helps to hold it firmly on the board using one of your hands while you finish your knot using the remaining hand.

Bring the tip by your bight above and below (from top to bottom).

To make the bight tight, tighten the section that is close to your bead. Tug on the tip to make the remaining part tight.

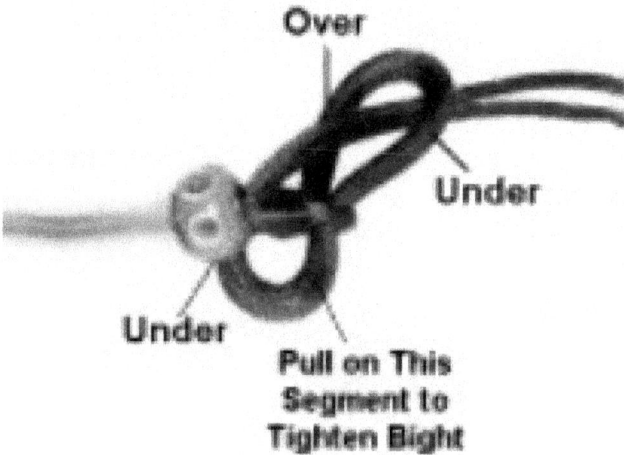

Step 5

Rework steps two to four a couple of times while you incorporate additional beads. Instead of finishing with a bead, use a knot.

When your bracelet reaches half of the length that you intend to make, stop. For instance, stop at three and a half inches for a finished bracelet of seven inches in length.

Ensure that all your oysterman knots are as close as possible to your beads. Where there's a lot of space, it becomes challenging to remove knots and backtracking.

Flip your bracelet over and return to the middle. What you should do first is tying a knot for buttons adjacent to your bead using the remaining half of your cord. Proceed on tying additional knots and incorporating extra beads until you get your bracelet to your required size. Ensure that you remember to finish with a knot and not a bead.

Step 6

To create the clasp, bring 2 cords from the same bracelet end through one bead. Repeat with the other side, but this time let them pass through in the opposite direction. To check the size, wear the macramé jewelry on the wrist; it is supposed to feel comfy with the tips pulled so that it is in the position for closing. If it is not the correct size, you might need to remove or add knots. To make your bracelet balanced, ensure that you do it on either end.

As you take off the bracelet, notice the distance that you need to slide the bead for your clasp to open it.

If it is past one and a half inches, as you execute the following step, position your knots further below on the tips.

Step 7

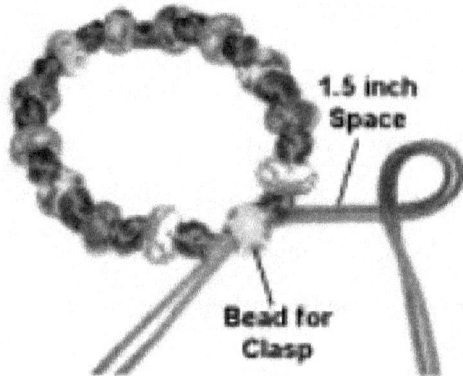

Leave out a minimum space of one and a half inches, then use the 2 ends to create an Oysterman knot. As you tighten it, apply glue so that it is inside of your knot.

If you wish, you may add extra glue on the exterior, although some types of glue will end up darkening your material. Therefore, before using the glue, test it out on a sheet of material scrap to avoid that.

Step 8:

Redo step seven using the remaining two ends. Allow the glue to dry before cutting off the additional material.

Filigree Bracelet

Let us put it all together. This last project uses many of the knots learned in the previous compositions. The Overhand knot, Flat knot, Alternating Lark's Head knot, and Diagonal Double Half Hitch knot are all in play here.

This "Lacelet" fits the very definition of filigree as it is both delicate and fanciful. I hope you enjoy this design that is open and light. The finished length is 7 1/2 inches and includes a button closure.

Knots Used:

- Overhand Knot

- Diagonal Double Half Hitch

- Flat Knot

- Alternating Lark's Head Knot

Supplies:

- 66" length white C-Lon cord, 4 strands

- 6 clear beads, 5mm

- 56 clear beads, 3mm

- 5 clear beads, 4mm

- 1 bead for button closure, about 7mm

- 164 clear seed beads

- Glue - Beacon 527 multi-use

Note: You can vary the bead sizes slightly. Just be sure the beads you choose will slide onto 2, and sometimes 3 cords. (The seed beads only need to fit onto one cord).

Instructions:

1. Find the center of the cords and lightly tie an overhand knot. Pin this onto your project board. Tie about 9 flat knots (for 7mm button closure bead). Now undo the overhand knot and fold the flat knots into a horseshoe shape. Using the outer cord from each side, tie 1 flat knot.

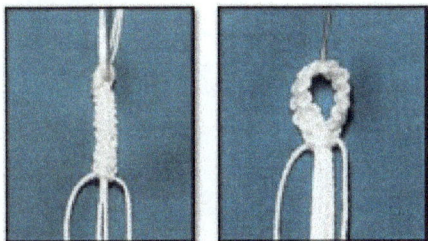

2. Take the rightmost cord and place it over all others down to the left to work Diagonal Double Half Hitch (DDHH) knots from right to left. Put 1 clear seed bead on each cord, then tie another set of DDHH knots from right to left.

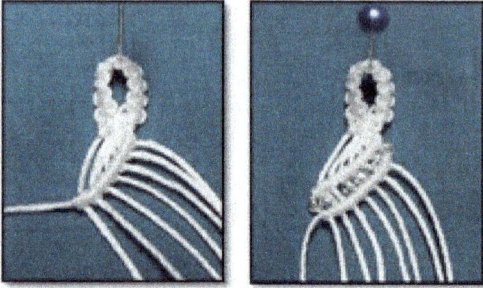

3. Separate cords into 4-4. Working with left 4 cords bead as follows: on the leftmost cord, put 4 clear 3mm beads with a seed bead between each one. The next cord gets 5 clear seed beads. The next cord needs a 5mm clear bead. And the last cord of this section gets 5 clear seed beads. Use the outer 2 cords to tie a flat knot around the inner cords.

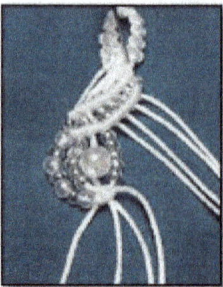

4. Working with right 4 cords: Place a 3mm clear bead on the center 2 cords. Place a seed bead on the rightmost cord. Now use this rightmost cord to tie an Alternating Lark's Head (ALH) knot around the other 3 cords. Repeat 4 times.

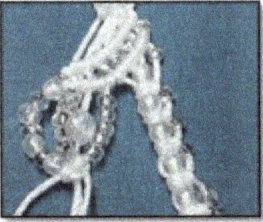

5. Using the leftmost cord as a holding cord, work DDHH knots from left to right. Place a seed bead on each cord, then work another set of DDHH knots (from left to right again) using the leftmost cord as your holding cord.

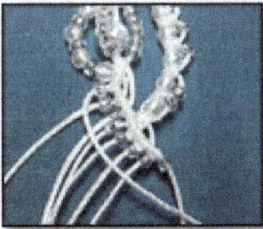

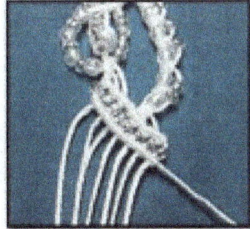

6. Separate cords into 4-4. Working with left 4 cords: Place a 3mm clear bead on the center 2 cords. Place a seed bead on the leftmost cord. Now use this left most cord to tie an ALH knot around the other 3 cords. Repeat 4 times.

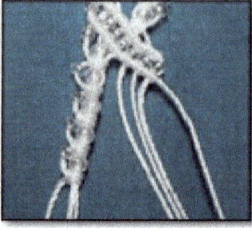

7. Working with the right 4 cords: the rightmost cord gets 4 clear 3mm beads with a seed bead between each one. The next cord in from the right needs 5 seed beads. The next cord in gets a 5mm clear bead. And the last cord of this section gets 5 seed beads. Use the outer 2 cords to tie a flat knot around the inner cords.

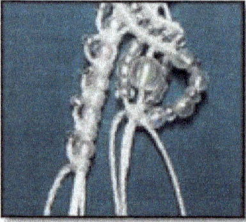

8. Repeat steps 2-7 for pattern until you have about 6 1/2 inches in length.

9. Separate cords into 3-2-3. On the left set of cords, place a 4mm bead. With the center 2 cords thread on a 3mm bead, a 4mm bead, and another 3mm bead. On the right 3 cords, place three 4mm beads. Find the outermost cord on each side and tie a flat knot around the rest.

10. Thread your button bead onto the center 4 or 6 cords if possible. Use the outer cords to tie a flat knot. Glue flat knot and let dry. Trim excess cords.

Nautical Rope Necklace

This one is light and easy on the eyes, and is quite edgy—literally and figuratively, without being over the top! It will also remind you of the sea—or the waves of the ocean!

What you need:

- Pendant with jump ring or bail
- Ruler
- Scissors
- White nylon cord
- Knotting board

Instructions:

Cut 7 feet or 84" of nylon cord.

Then, keep the strands together as a group. Tie an overhand knot around the two strings. Make sure there's 1 to 2" of space between them.

Make an overhand knot 6" away from the end. Tighten the knot by pulling individual strands and make sure to secure it on the knotting board. Separate the strands into two groups.

Take the left part of the cord and cross it under the right corner of the cord. Get the right cord group and cross it over the left side. Tighten as you pull down and knot until you reach 16 inches.

Check the last double chain and make an overhand knot. Tie them 6 inches from what you have created. Add a pendant, if you want, and make sure you knot before and after adding it to keep it secure.

Macrame Glass Connector Bracelet

Supplies

You need approximately 3 m of glass connectors and cords for each bracelet. I chose the 2 mm string, but you can use 1 mm (although I strongly suggest it should be 1,5 mm longer at least).

Instructions

For the first time, let's make the bracelet.

Take a 20 cm piece and slip it over the connector leg.

1. Take the 1 m piece and tie your knot middle. You have two lines now, one to the left and one to the right.

2. Take the right string and slide it into the middle string and into the left string.

3. Take the left thread, slip it on the center string, then close the knot under the left string.

4. Repeat the steps until on one hand you make the bracelet. Finally cut off those ends and then burn them to melt and stick and make the other leg. When you tie the knots, a spiral is formed. It's going to feel like that.

Switch to the second form now. Steps 1, 2, 3 are the same for this method as the first step.

The difference is that you don't repeat the same move repeatedly!

After tying the first leg, slip the left cord under the cords in the center and over the right cord over the center and left cords.

Tie the knot, which looks like 2 knots.

Alternately tie the ties on either hand until the desired length is reached. Repeat the other side of the bracelet.

Change your bracelets with another short cord and the second option instead of a clasp. Combine both ends and tie the knots on both ends.

Macramé Tie-Dye Necklace 1

This one is knotted tightly, which gives it the effect that it's strong—but still really elegant. This is a good project to craft—you'd enjoy the act of making it, and wearing it, as well!

What you need:

- 1 pack laundry rope
- Tulip One-Step Dye
- Fabric glue
- Candle
- Jump rings
- Lobster clasp

Instructions:

Tie the rope using crown knots.

After tying, place the knotted rope inside the One-Step Dye pack (you could get this in most stores) and let it set and dry overnight.

Upon taking it out, leave it for a few hours and then secure the end of the knot with fabric glue mixed with a bit of water.

Trim the ends off and burn off the ends with wax from candle.

Add jump rings to the end and secure with lobster clasp.

Enjoy your tie-dye necklace!

Knotted Chevron Headband

Materials:

- Broder floss (6 colors/12 suits my 1/2-inch wide headband)

- The satin narrow belt – 1/8 to 1/4 "is perfect.

- E6000 or equivalent adhesive plastic

- 1/2 centimeter long or your favorite headband

- Matched thread and needle sewing

Steps:

Start by making your new long friendship bracelet. I've been using 6 strands each 10 feet in length, half by 5 feet, but if your headband is more extensive, maybe your headband would be more significant. Hold a loose knot together and tie the strands and operate the Classic Chevron Friendship Bracelet (or pattern for you) until the strip is 1 to 5 inches longer than the length of the headband. Untie the knot upon completion.

Get a dot of glue on the back of your headband and put it around your headband. Make sure you cover the band on the front and back, and if you have a single face on the satin belt, the right side is off. Cut off the tails one end of the knitted strip and hold it down. Save it for a few minutes. Put some glue on your back and tie the knotted strip to the rope until it is imperfect. So go on gluing and binding, but then behind the knotted thread. Avoid gluing and wrapping when the knotted strip is as far away from the other end. Cut the tails to the end and add the whole length of the super long bracelet to the end. Likely, you will extend it a little to match, and that's perfect. (Keep it to the end only if you want to stitch the kneaded portion on the back). Hold on to the end of the strip and tie it smoothly on your back to the end of the headband. When you just hang up, you can thread the knotted piece back and forth on the edges and draw it close. This is the right choice because the line has very straight edges.

Conclusion

Macramé has been innovated in recent decades, and with it, any decorative instrument can be made, curtains, tapestries, wall hangings, tablecloths, cushions, and quilts. Just anything you can think of to decorate. Also, with the macramé, you can make any accessory you want.

Even this book has brought you a small guide to some of the simplest projects to carry out so that you can get to work. Now it only remains to start in this fantastic world.

You will be knotting your way to beautiful bits in no time.

Nowadays, macramé hobby and ability mean different things to different people. The skill is useful for many in a variety of ways. Tying the various knots will strengthen arms and hands. It can be very soothing to the mind, body, and spirit to build a macramé project!

There are more and more options for superior macramé to improve the decor of your house, wardrobe, and personal style for those who just want to use and enjoy the finished pieces. To decide a period of time it will take to learn how to macramé depends on various factors, such as how easily you will learn this technique. If you have been knitting or sewing for a long time, the degree of difficulty will be slightly lower, as there are some parallels with the process.

You should pursue the above-described beginner projects, or if you want to, you can also search online for other macramé projects as there are several kinds of stuff you can do, but you must know how to macramé first. You will find numerous tips and videos on the internet for that too. When you have learned the simple stitching, use macramé, you can do anything you want!

CPSIA information can be obtained
at www.ICGtesting.com
Printed in the USA
BVHW091529180321
602886BV00003B/530

9 781801 589901